MY Family's Story

the Connollys

My Story is about My Great-Grandfather Cornelius O'Mahony

1916

My ... from ...

Micheal John Mclean!

IRELANDS FIGHT FOR FREEDOM

A Project About Richard O'Neill Irish Volunteer

The Big house burings in County Cork during the Irish Revolution.

OUR GREAT-GRANDAD!

Independence Story By Cork Helbrow

Lieutenant John Connolly 1894 - 1920

My great grand uncle Jeremiah Walsh

Family History of the Rising

My Great-Grandmothers Memories of the Kilmichael Ambush

MY PROJECT ON MY GREAT GREAT GRANDFATHER THOMAS CROWLEY

My Unknown Hero

THE STORY

CHARLES McCarthy 1901 - 1987

MY GREAT GRANDAD BARRETT

Stories of the Revolution

'I have learnt so much from this project and read how so many poor innocent families suffered. We should all be kind to each other and be grateful that there is no war going on in Ireland today.'

Molly Hilliard, Coppeen National School.

Stories
of the
Revolution

Terri Kearney & Margaret Murphy

STORIES OF THE REVOLUTION

First published in 2022 by:
Macalla Publishing,
Cunnamore,
Skibbereen, West Cork, Ireland.
macallapublishing@gmail.com

ISBN: 978-0-9926242-4-8

Cover photos: Kevin O'Farrell Photographer

Images inside front cover by:
Rachel Crowley, St Joseph's National School, Dromore I Sam & Ben Jones, Kilcolman National School I Grace O'Neill, Gurraneasig National School I Gavin O'Sullivan, St Joseph's National School, Dromore I Gavin Nyhan, Kilcolman National School I Caoimhe Burns, St Mary's Senior School, Dunmanway I Aoife O'Flynn Meade, Kilcolman National School I Joshua & Emily Williamson, Knockskeagh National School I Jack & Tadg Crowley, Dreeny National School I Tadhg Ó Seighin, Gaelscoil Mhichíl Uí Choileáin, Clonakilty I Darragh Ó Mathúna, Gaelscoil Mhichíl Uí Choileáin, Clonakilty I Derry Ó Donnabháin, Gaelscoil Mhichíl Uí Choileáin, Clonakilty I Denis Cadogan, St Joseph's National School, Dromore I Saoirse Horgan, St Joseph's National School, Dromore I Katie Scannell, St Joseph's GNS, Skibbereen I Suzie Murphy, Scoil Eoin National School, Innishannon I Aoife d'Hondt, St Joseph's National School, Dromore I Caoimhe & Maebh McCarthy, St Mary's Senior School, Dunmanway I Eimer Martin, St Mary's Senior School, Dunmanway I Claire & Ella Dromey, Dromleigh National School I Matthew O'Neill, Scoil Phádraig Naofa, Dunmanway Connor Crowley, St Joseph's National School, Dromore I Daisy Bean, Gaelscoil Dhroichead na Banndan I Greg Mulhall, St Joseph's National School, Dromore I Eoin Hurley, Scoil Phádraig Naofa, Dunmanway I Orlaith O'Flynn Meade, Kilcolman National School I Aoife Galvin, Kilcolman National School I Raonaid Kerrisk, Leap National School I Carly Helbrow, Ballinadee National School I Liam Henry Kearney, Scoil Phádraig Naofa, Dunmanway I Killian Collins, Scoil Phádraig Naofa, Dunmanway I Lily O'Donnell Bradley, Gaelscoil Mhichíl Uí Choileáin, Clonakilty I Nicholas Curtin, Scoil Eoin National School, Innishannon.

Design and Layout: Alan Tobin and Terri Kearney

Edited by: Flor MacCarthy

Printed in Ireland. **S** | SOUTHERN STAR
CREATIVE

Contents

Foreword

'Posterity! You will never know, how much it cost the present Generation to preserve your Freedom! I hope you will make good use of it.'

John Adams, 1777.

'Revolution' means change. Change is very often a slow process but sometimes it can be accelerated as a result of political pressure, natural disaster, disease or war. History is a record of change and every person supplies a thread to the rich tapestry of history. Family life, school days, work life, church celebrations, fairs, markets, all make up our social history. Social change and political change are symbiotic, as evinced by the revolutionary period in Ireland, 1916-1923. Slowly, the mindset of the majority of the population moved towards embracing the idea of an independent Irish Republic. This idea percolated down from a revolutionary elite from 1798 through the 19th century and finally crystallised in the fire of the 1916 Rising and its aftermath. Irish self determination became a demand, as Sinn Féin swept the boards in the 1918 General Election, standing on a platform of abstention from Westminster and the creation of an Irish Republic. For many of the people who cast their ballots in that election, it was their first time doing so, the franchise having recently been extended to include all men over the age of 21 and some property-owning women over the age of 30. In spite of the democratic mandate for an Irish Republic, violence was also used to redouble the demand. And so, just as the people of Ireland acted, the British government reacted with a determined campaign to extinguish the flame of Republicanism resulting in a bloody war.

The voters and Volunteers of that time, over one hundred years ago, would now have great-grandchildren of primary school age. This project, whereby children were encouraged to ask their parents and grandparents about any anecdotes or stories that they remember being told about that time, truly is important. It ensures that the school pupils of today, the voting citizens of tomorrow, will really understand the price that was paid by earlier generations to gain and preserve their freedom. This method of historical inquiry, of going back as closely as possible to the source, to peel back the layers of modernity and to understand the motives of those who fought and the impact of war on the lives of all people at the time, is an invaluable introduction to research for the pupils of the primary schools of West cork who took part in this project. I commend the pupils, the teachers, the family members who supplied the stories and in particular, Terri Kearney and Margaret Murphy and the rest of the Skibbereen Heritage Centre team, and my fellow Councillors on Cork County Council's Commemorations Committee for supporting this excellent project. As Mayor, it is my privilege to attend and to speak at many commemorations around the County. I always give a special welcome to children because it is they who will bear witness to these events to future generations. This production encourages that youthful curiosity and will lead to further insight and understanding, traits we will need in the leaders of the future. All of the pupils involved in this project are already making 'good use' of the freedom and rights won for them, over one hundred years ago.

Maith sibh as an éacht iontach atá bainte amach agaibh agus beirigí bua!

Mayor of Cork County, Cllr Gillian Coughlan, June 2022.

About The Project

Participants and organisers at the 2017 Awards Ceremony held at Skibbereen Community school.

The genesis of 'The Stories of the Revolution' project dates back to 2015 and, like many a good idea, it was inspired by a strong cup of coffee. Modelled on the highly successful schools' folklore programme of 1937, it invited local children to record oral history from the older community about the 1916-23 revolutionary period, and to submit these stories in the form of essays.

The concept was embraced wholeheartedly by the Skibbereen Heritage Centre team, kindly enabled by funding from the Cork County Council Centenary programme, and the pupils and teachers of the participating schools were equally enthusiastic about their involvement in the project.

Over four years, the project team visited 48 schools in the greater West Cork area, covering the Skibbereen, Clonakilty, Bandon and Dunmanway districts. Unfortunately we were unable to extend it over subsequent years to other areas as planned, due to the global pandemic. However, in those few years, the project still managed to involve 823 children, garnering just short of 800 essays, some containing multiple stories, most of which were previously unrecorded.

This publication contains extracts from just some of these wonderful essays and represents only a tiny fraction of the overall project. Thankfully, due to Cork County Council's ongoing support, the entire collection can be enjoyed online on the Skibbereen Heritage Centre website www. skibbheritage.com. The original hard copies of the projects will also form a 'Stories of the Revolution' archive at the Cork City and County Archives Institute, where they will be preserved for posterity.

Speaking on behalf of the Skibbereen Heritage Centre team, we can truly say that we are thrilled to have undertaken this worthwhile project. Both the participants and organisers gained so much from it (see the 'PS from the kids' chapter), and we now also have this invaluable collection of oral history as a result too.

Our only regret is that we cannot feature every single essay in this publication, but we hope that it will prompt readers to go to the online database to browse the collection in full. And we know that you will love reading these wonderful stories just as much as we so enjoyed the process of collecting them.

Terri Kearney & Margaret Murphy, June 2022.

Overall Winning Pupil in 2017, Katie Scannell (St Joseph's GNS, Skibbereen) with Gavin Kiely, Access Credit Union (inaugural year prize sponsor) and Cllr Mary Hegarty (deputising for the Cork County Mayor) at the Awards Ceremony.

Pupils from Leap National School, the overall Winning School in 2017, with Mary Crowley (principal/teacher) and Carolyn O'Neill (SNA), with Cllr Mary Hegarty (deputising for the Cork County Mayor) at the Awards Ceremony. Also in the photo: Gavin Kiely and Mary Crowley of Access Credit Union (inaugural year prize sponsor) and Cllr Joe Caroll; Cork County Council Heritage Officer Conor Nelligan; and the Skibbereen Heritage Centre team, Sue Harrington, Terri Kearney, Philip O'Regan, Margaret Murphy and Deirdre Collins.

Mayor of Cork County, Cllr Declan Hurley with pupils from Scoil Eoin National School, Innishannon, the overall Winning School at the 2018 Awards Ceremony. Also included in the photo are Scoil Eoin principal and teachers, Aoife Finn, Carol Ní Chuimín and Emma Crowley; Cllr Alan Coleman and Cork County Council Heritage Officer Conor Nelligan with Terri Kearney, Philip O'Regan and Margaret Murphy of Skibbereen Heritage Centre.

Mayor of Cork County, Cllr Declan Hurley, with the overall Winning Pupil Kevin Dart-O'Flynn at Scoil Eoin National School, Innishannon in 2018.

Mayor of Cork County Cllr Patrick Gerard Murphy with Eoin Hurley, the overall Winning Pupil at Scoil Phádraig Naofa, Dunmanway in 2019. Also in the photo: Conor Nelligan, Niall Healy and Mac Dara O h-Icí of Cork County Council: and Skibbereen Heritage Centre team members, William Casey, Margaret Murphy and Terri Kearney.

Mayor of Cork County Cllr Patrick Gerard Murphy with pupils of Dromleigh National School, the 2019 overall Winning School, with teacher/principal Anne Bradley. Also in the photo: Conor Nelligan, Niall Healy and Mac Dara O h-Icí of Cork County Council; and Skibbereen Heritage Centre team members William Casey, Margaret Murphy, Sue Harrington and Terri Kearney.

Mayor of Cork County in 2020, Cllr Ian Doyle, presenting the prizes to the overall Winning Pupil, Lily O'Donnell Bradley of Gaelscoil Mhichíl Uí Choileáin, Clonakilty and teacher Seán Ó Duinnín, accepting the Winning School prize that year on behalf of Gaelscoil Mhichíl Uí Choileáin. Also in the photo are Clodagh Henehan and Niall Healy of Cork County Council.

Mayor of Cork County in 2020, Cllr Ian Doyle, with participating teachers Seán Ó Duinnín, Caitríona Ní Mhurchu and Fionnuala Ní Chonchubhair from Gaelscoil Mhichíl Uí Choileáin, Clonakilty, the overall Winning School that year. Also in the photo: principal Padraig Ó hEachthairn, deputy principal Íde Ní Mhuirí and chairperson Traolach Ó Donnabhain with the overall Winning Pupil that year, Lily O'Donnell Bradley, also a student at that school.

Introduction

'Collect the fragments,
lest they perish.'

Folklore of Ireland Society, 1927

On the day that my mother was born, 28 November 1920, another little girl 40 miles away crouched under a table as bullets ricocheted off the walls of her home in Kilmichael.

Nell Kelly was just 12 years old when Tom Barry came to her family's door that morning, telling them to 'stay indoors and keep away from the windows'. A surprise attack on British forces was to take place on the road outside later that day, and 'from 8am to 4pm, Nell and her family were held in their own home'. After the ambush, the family were forced to flee as their family home was 'burned to the ground'.

'[The family] had to run as fast as they could, Nell lost her shoe on the way and wasn't allowed back. Connie said to her dying day she would say that as a result of the Kilmichael Ambush she had lost her good confirmation shoe.' [1]

The site of the Kilmichael Ambush is now marked with a commemorative monument and many more such memorials are dotted around the Irish landscape, bearing witness to the turbulent birth of our nation. But each of these locations also has a rich intangible legacy — fragile fragments of memory, and an emotional inheritance that still holds sway today.

'Kathy rarely wanted to talk of the Kilmichael Ambush as it caused great trauma to all involved. They were so traumatised and upset to see bodies lying dead on the road … [and] they were heartbroken to see their three friends dead.' [2]

Revolution affects an entire population, especially so when guerrilla tactics and civil war are involved. But many of the intimate experiences of that era remain hidden from our 'official' history, concealed in the folds of family lore and the confines of the immediate locality.

'My granny's dad was not allowed to see his mother in her own house because of politics. My grandfather could only see his mother in the sister's house because the brother lived with the mother and could not go in because they would have a fight about Michael Collins and Éamon deValera.' [3]

This rich tapestry of inherited memory is in danger of being lost now as those who grew up in the shadow of 'the troubles' fade away. So the children who participated in this project and their interviewees have done us a great service in recording these personal accounts — including Nell Kelly's great-grandson Eoin who has so eloquently documented his ancestor's recollections of that fateful day in 1920.

'As the [Kelly] house was so close to the action, bullets flew in … After the shooting stopped, Tom Barry returned to the house looking to remove the doors for stretchers for the dead and dying.' [4]

Many of the children's stories are about ordinary people trying to get on with their everyday lives in a time of war. It was a 'hard time to live' when both sides could 'randomly barge in' and commandeer their scarce resources at gunpoint. And they lived under the constant threat of being shot too. But still local people fell in love, worked their farms and buried their dead despite the violence playing out around them.

'My great grandad had put away a pair of shoes in Grant's Shoe Shop for his wedding day. The Black and Tans burnt down Cork the day before [the] wedding. The best man went down to collect the shoes but the shop had been burnt and looted and all he could get was one black and one brown shoe. It did not bring [them] any bad luck as they had 17 children and lived a long and happy life together.' [5]

But we have numerous testimonies from those directly involved in the struggle too, of raids, bombings, executions and kidnappings. An account of Michael Collins' last night; Dev's immediate reaction to Collins' shooting; and a Cumann na mBan member's respect for the Englishwoman playing Rule Britannia on piano as the building around her burned — personal stories that offer a unique perspective of these 'big history' events.

'During the Civil War when Michael Collins was shot, Jack was driving Éamon deValera in an area outside Fermoy … When they received news from an oncoming motorbike that the "Big Fellow" was shot, DeValera put his hands to his face and started to cry and said "Poor Mick, poor Mick".' [6]

It truly was a time of chaos and terror, with the widespread fear and loathing of the British 'Black and Tans' still palpable today in these essays. Raids, random shootings, and drunken soldiers running riot appear repeatedly throughout the collection, the trauma of their brutal actions still echoing through the collective memory.

'[The Black and Tans] began burning houses and firing shots at people and houses. My great grandmother [aged 6] remembers being really frightened and her mother hid her and her siblings in the fireplace so they wouldn't get hurt by stray bullets or glass. They burned down 13 houses that night and killed two people.' [7]

The essays also tell us a lot about the logistical challenges involved in guerrilla warfare — from the bogs, biscuits tins and coffins used to cache arms, to the many ingenious ways of smuggling secret messages, and the day-to-day operation of safe houses. And there are tales of tragedy too — the young IRA man shot in the back as he fled a safe house; 'brother fighting against brother' during the Civil War; and the RIC officer who was given a piece of his own wedding cake by 'kind strangers' before his execution.

Stories of the Revolution 1916 – 1923

'My great grandad's [family home] was a safe house … on cold, wet nights [he] and his sisters were woken out of their sleep to give their beds to the Irish soldiers. [His] mum would put on a fire and start baking brown bed … The soldiers took brown bread and glass bottles of tea with them when they left … covered with a hand-knitted sock to keep them warm. My great grandad and his family would say the rosary when they left for their safety.' [8]

Oral history deepens our understanding of the past and this is only amplified by the children's clear-eyed interpretation of these often-traumatic events. Some expressed their appreciation of the sacrifices made 'to pave the way to make a better life for us' while others were grateful that 'there is no war going on in Ireland today', and there are several sage comments about the futility of war — all proof, should we need it, that 'history is important' and that such projects are worthwhile.

'Only 3 of the 11 people that were killed were remembered on this monument — makes you wonder about the other innocent civilians who were killed that day going about their normal daily tasks. While we look back on these troubled times let's think about the innocent people and thank God for peace in Ireland.' [9]

Much has been written about this period on a national and international basis but, in real terms, each one of us experiences our life history as an individual, or as part of our local community. So, in that sense, local history fundamentally provides the building blocks of world history. While geography and chance dictated the content of this collection, these brief fragments certainly enrich our understanding of this pivotal period in history, and the children have done outstanding work collecting them.

We are delighted to record this precious material for future generations, and we hope someday that it will be valued and appreciated as the 1937 Schools' Folklore Collection is today. And everyone involved in this project is truly honoured to be part of that worthy endeavour.

'It was a very troubled time in Ireland and lucky my great grandad survived that stuff.' [10]

Terri Kearney, June 2022.

1. Lucia Duarte, Ambushes, p. 138.
2. Anna Goyal, ibid, p. 140.
3. Maebh Collins, Civil War, p. 153.
4. Eoin Hurley, Ambushes, p. 133.
5. Katie Scannell, Everyday Life, p. 19.
6. Kevin Dart-O'Flynn, IRA, p. 85.
7. Alaia O'Sullivan, Black and Tans, p. 36.
8. Gavin O'Sullivan, Safe Houses, p. 114.
9. Fiona Twohig, PS from the Kids, p. 181.
10. Alice Barrett, ibid, p. 180.
11. Ava Scarlett, Leap National School.

Tara O'Farrell
Scoil Eoin National School, Innishannon.

Adam Gilman-Burke
St Joseph's National School, Dromore.

Chapter 1

EVERYDAY LIFE

From the threat of being 'shot by accident' to the hardship of having their scarce resources commandeered by both sides, 1916-23 was a 'hard time to live' for ordinary people trying to go about their daily lives.

Niamh Quinlan
Scoil Naomh Seosamh, Laragh.

List of Names

Ava Scarlett
Leap National School.

During those years came another rule. Every family had to have a list of names of the people in the house, which they had to keep inside the front door. If the Black and Tans found another person in the house, whose name was not on the list, they would have been shot. Donal told us a story about a man named Con who was on the run. He stayed at "a safe house" in Carrigfada for the night. The family didn't put his name on the list. The man slept in one of the son's beds. The woman of the house heard a lorry, she called Con and he escaped through a small back window of the house. When the Black and Tans came, they questioned the son who had been sleeping in the same bed as Con. The Black and Tans knew because the bed had been too warm for just one body. The son said he had been sleeping with his sister. The Black and Tans laughed at the thought of a middle aged man sleeping with his sister. Fortunatley he got away with it.

Imprisoned … for six months

As O.C. Skibbereen Battalion Samuel Kingston became a person of interest to the R.I.C. Samuel's fathers house was raided in December 1920 looking for Samuel. The house was torn asunder. His father Paul and brother William (my Great-grandad) were taken away for not having the names of the occupants up on the door. They were taken to Dunmanway and then to Bandon. His father was fined £5. William was taken to Spike Island as Paul was to old and frail to go there. William was imprisoned there for a period of six months.

Katie Kingston
Dreeny National School.

Curfew:

From 1916 to 1923 there was a curfew. People had to stay inside their houses between 10 pm at night and 6 am next morning. If you were outside between 10 pm and 6 am the patrollers (The Black and Tans) could shoot you on the spot.

Ava Scarlett
Leap National School.

Cillian Cuffe
Gurrane National School.

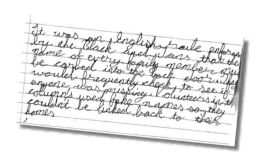

'It was an English rule enforced by the Black and Tans that the name of every family member must be carved into the back door. They would frequently check to see if anyone was missing. Volunteers in the columns used fake names so they couldn't be linked back to their homes'

Matthew Hoban
Scoil Mhaoilíosa, Knockavilla.

Clár Ní Ríordáin
Gaelscoil Dhroichead na Banndan.

Lá amháin bhí mo sin-seanmháthair ag seasamh ag an doras Bhí geansaí rua glas aici ansin Saighdiúrí ó sassana agus duirt siad chun an geansaí a bhaint. Thóg an saighdiúrí é agus scríoch siad é mar bhí sé glas.

Once my great Grandad had to drive his cattle (from Bunalun out from Skibbereen) with 3 or 4 men.

Though it was not so simple. They had to do it at the dead of night or they (and the cattle) would be shot. Some IRA members would shoot without questioning and some would question. Luckily he never ever got caught. On the way to Bandon, Skibbereen and Dunmanway (where the fairs were) they would hide under bridges to get rest. It would take 2 or 3 nights

We are nearly there

Told to Matthew Benn by Elizabeth Benn My Granny

Matthew Benn
Abbeystrewry National School, Skibbereen.

THE BURNING OF CORK

The Two Odd Shoes:
My Grandad Patrick Scannell's dad (My Great Grandad) Daniel Scannell had put away a pair of black shoes in Grants Shoe Shop for his Wedding Day. On the 11th of December 1920 the Black n Tans burnt down Cork the day before my Great Grandad's Wedding. The best man

Katie Scannell
St Joseph's GNS, Skibbereen.

went down to collect the shoes but the shop had been burnt and looted and all he could get was one black and one brown shoe. His mother got a tin of black shoe polish and tried polishing the brown shoe black. It did not bring my Great Grandad Scannell and Great nannie Scannell any bad luck as they had 17 children and lived a long and happy life together.
My Great Grandad Daniel was 6 foot 2 inch tall and My Great nannie Molly was 5 foot tall. He used to pick her up and swing her around like a doll! My Great nannie Scannell wore a powder blue suit on her Wedding Day.

2.

My Great-gran-aunt was brought a lovely doll. from the burning of Cork by a black and tan soildier.

Caoimhe & Maebh McCarthy
St Mary's Senior School, Dunmanway.

Chased by 'Tan

Great granny Madge

'One day my great granny who's name was Margaret, was pushing my great aunt, Hilda in a buggy. She saw a British soldier on the side of the road with his gun. Of course she was petrified and hurried along the road. She had just walked past him, when he started to shout and run after her. She ran as fast as her legs could carry her and the soldier probably wouldn't have caught up to her if she hadn't been pushing a buggy. He eventually ran in front of her and stopped her.

"I am a father myself", he said. "And I know that one sock is no good on its own".

He was holding up a little pink sock that had fallen off my great gran aunt Hilda's foot!'

Jonah Sutton
Kilgarriffe National School.

Just talking about greyhounds

Naomi Evans
Abbeystrewry National School, Skibbereen.

Ella O'Sullivan,
Dreeny National School.

One day Jack went to visit Lil's brother. Lil's brother also owned greyhounds so they were just talking about greyhounds as you would. They talked for a while then Jack went home.

Later on that evening it was announced that Jack was to be shot because of something he said that morning but he really didn't say anything that would get him into trouble.

Everyone was so scared. Jack was thinking of going hiding out in a neighbour's house but the next morning of the day he was going to be shot it was announced that he wasn't to be shot and that was because Lil's brother met with the leader of the I.R.A and told him that Jack was not to be shot as he didn't say anything wrong. He was just talking about greyhounds with him. So in the end Jack did not end up being shot and Lil's brother saved Jack! The End!

This is a picture of Mary who got a bullet in the leg.

'My other great, great grandmother Mary Doran was walking home from work. Then she got caught in the cross [fire] between Ireland and the Black and Tans and she got shot in the leg. … She was also very lucky because she got dragged in by a woman into a doorway and they looked after her.'

Leah Carey
Kilcoe National School.

Annabel Tapia
Kilcolman National School.

Shot by accident

The people called Black and Tans always want to catch Irish people and always had their guns ready to shoot. This man called Tim Whooley was in Shannon Vale climbing a fence. The Black and Tans didn't see him or shoot him. One of their guns went off by accident and shot Tim Whooley. The gun was one of the Black and Tans. So now people say Tim Whooley was shoot by accident by climbing a fence

'My great grandad John Tomas Coppinger, told mum when she was a little girl about the Black and Tan soldiers that were sent to Ireland by the English army to control Irish people during the rebellion. They used to raid Irish homes and cause trouble. They would raid great grandad's house and sometimes great grandad's parents had puteen to get money and pay for good land. Great grandad's mum and dad said to him to get in to bed and rub powder on your face and pretend to be ill so when he got to bed his parents slid the puteen under the blankets next to John and when the Black and Tans came in and raided the house they wouldn't know that they had puteen in the bed.'

Thalia McGuigan
Gaelscoil Dhochtúir Uí Shúilleabháin, An Sciobairín.

The thrashing

In October 1920 my Great-Great Grand Father was in Ballinascarthy at a thrashing and he had beer in the back of the horse and cart when suddenly, a few British soldiers came up to him and asked him what he had in the back.

He then replied that he had milk in the back because he did not want to admit that he was bringing alcohol to the trashing because they would probably steal the bottles of beer and drink it themselves.

The soldier then replied "Mulk?". The British army then frightened the horse and the horse bolted and he fell off the horse and cart and broke his leg and then he had a limp in his legs for the rest of his life.

Martha Coakley
Ballinadee National School.

Demanded his horse

Molly O'Brien
The Model School, Dunmanway.

'My great, great grandfather William O'Brien was coming home on the Inch road from Dromleena bog, when he was met by two Black and Tans with three horses. They demanded his horse and load of turf which he had collected from the bog earlier that day. He pleaded with them not to take his horse so he could get home safely.

The Black and Tans agreed, but they still took his horsecar, and load of turf. As the Black and Tans had a third horse, they used it to take the horsecar of turf back to the Barrack in Macroom.

Three months later, the Irish guards called to my great, great grandfather's farm and asked him had his turf been taken by the Black and Tans, because they heard that the Black and Tans had been stealing in the area. My great, great grandfather said "no" because he was grateful that the Black and Tans let him keep his horse.'

Around 1920, Paddy's father (Michael) and uncles were living in Myross Island. One uncle, Pat, owned a house and farm in Bawnlahan also. There was a crop called mangles, which was a bit like beet growing there and in November two of Paddy's uncles, Peter & Tom were sent up to this farm to draw in the mangles before the frost which would destroy the crop.

The Black & Tans arrived at the house and lined up the two uncles to be shot, thinking they were the other 2 brothers, Pat & Michael, who were on the run at the time.

A drunken policeman came along and informed the Tans that they weren't the right 2 brothers. The lads were left off but the Tans burned the house.

Saved by drunken policeman

Paddy French, Sarah McCarthy
& Liadhain Hogan
Scoil Naomh Bhríde, Union Hall.

My Grandad's aunt died and they were having a wake (funeral) at her house in Camus. That evening when the Black and tans saw a large gathering of people at the house, they thought that the people that were gathered were planning an ambush. So, they got their armour and planned an attack on the house. However one of the local neighbours passing by, stopped them and informed them that funeral was taking place

Daniel, Euan & Kate Whelton
S.N Rath A' Bharraigh/Rathbarry National School.

Lucija Kluzniak Madajczak
Abbeystrewry National School, Skibbereen.

Paul's grandmother Charlotte Dowling, was around 16, when her father sadly died. The whole family gathered to bury him. It was planned to happen on Monday, wich was Easter Monday that year. But one of her brothers, who was a member of the Volunteers, heard from one of his coleuges that it would be wiser to bury his father on Sunday, even though that was strangely, unusual, because something "BIG" was going to happen. What he didn't know, was that the Rising was planned for Easter Monday.
So Paul's great grandfather, was buried on Easter Sunday in Harold's cross, in Dublin.
It was a thirstily hot day and Paul's grandmother remembered it all. Fantastic how mind's work....

Danny Buckley's sister Mary came under sustained rifle fire as she cycled home from mass and was probably saved by the intervention of a hostage, being carried by troops, who brought to their attention that they were firing on a woman. He also recalled numbers of strange men sleeping in his bedroom on occasions and rows of rifles propped up against the wall. He further recalled the Civil war period and being in Renanirree school when a party of Free State Troops, commanded by John L. O'Sullivan, were engaged by Republicans at Renanirree church, close by the school. The pupils were ordered to lie on the floor, by the walls, as many bullets came through the windows.

These were some of the experiences of a child during the historic and troubled times.

Isabel Nic Suibhne
Gaelscoil Dhochtúir Uí Shúilleabháin, An Sciobairín.

Bullets through windows

During those times when the Black and Tans and the auxiliaries were raiding the countryside, people were advised to bury any valuables such as silver and jewellery as the British forces were known to take items of value. They had stores set up in England where they could sell these stolen goods. During that time also many people had timber shutters inside the windows to protect themselves from bullets. It was never safe to sit in front of the window.

James & Catherine O'Callaghan
Leap National School.

'When the IRA needed to transport messages or guns, they used children. As Maureen looked sweet and innocent, she was the perfect walking disguise. She and her sisters carried guns under their skirts and petticoats. If, for example, one of the IRA received a tipoff that one of their safe-houses was to be raided, they would notify the children of the village. Then the children would meander over, with various excuses. The children went in with missions, they came out with guns. Maureen never suspected a thing. She enjoyed the "game" and only found out when she was older. She had the biggest adventure of her life and didn't realise it.'

Lucie Bradley
Kilgarriffe National School.

An Unexpected Order

Patrick 'Pa' Gallagher was born in 1888 in Ballyhenda Fermoy, Co.Cork. He had 2 sisters and 5 brothers. When he finished school he moved to Dublin for work. He worked in Sinlaters Groceries. One Sunday morning in 1914 he was walking by Howth Bay, when he was held at gunpoint by a rebel and ordered to unload The Asgard. The Asgard was owned by English born and Irish nationalist Erskine Childers and his wife Molly. It had a cargo of 900 guns and 2,900 rounds of ammunition. There was alot of witnesses there and Pa was afraid he would be recognised so he left Dublin and returned to Fermoy.

Forced to unload the Asgard

Eimer Martin
St Mary's Senior School, Dunmanway.

A Knock on the Door

My Grandfather was born in 1916. He was only about four or five when the Black and Tans came to his door. He was so scared that he hid under the table. His Mom and Dad were really scared too. If I was there I would have run away.

Emer Moroney
Kilcolman National School.

Gráinne Connolly
Rathmore National School.

Eileen Coughlan also told me this story about her father Jim O'Brien. He was a small farmer and had hay in cocks in a field close to the road. He was turning the hay when he heard the Black and Tans coming down the road, walking. He decided to hide from them so that they would not ask him to help them. They did not see him. He was so frightened he thought the Black and Tans would hear his heart pounding. They didn't notice him and luckily moved on.

'During the trouble times of 1921-22 members of the IRA used to come looking for food and lodgings or a drive in a horse and cart. One particular night they had a very frightening experience when they were in bed the leader of a band of IRA men came to the front door demanding food and a place to sleep. They made it clear there was no choice but to accept them as one of them pushed the barrel of his rifle against the ceiling where my great grandmother slept as a child. Later that night my great grandmother's father Tim had to tackle the horse and cart and drive the men in the Bantry direction. My great grandmother Maryann, her brother Joe and mother thought they would never see their father again. They feared that they would be caught by the Black and Tans. Finally after a long wait, they heard the sound of the horse's hooves on the stone surface road making his way home. Their anxious wait was over when he returned safely. My great grandmother never forgot this 'till the day she died my grandaunt Theresa Hickey Coronea and my granduncle Tim Cadogan Galway tells me.'

Cathal O'Sullivan
Caheragh National School.

Ava Scarlett
Leap National School.

One night in 1920 Dan O'Donovan recalls that when the family had all gone to bed they heard some commotion in the farmyard, but when they looked out they saw nothing.

Next morning, as normal when the cows were milked, they went to get the horse and cart to bring the milk to the creamery but the cart was missing. They soon discovered that their neighbours cart was missing too. Later that morning they located the two carts. The iron rims had been taken off. The carts had been used to block the road so that when the R.I.C. or the Black and Tans would come, the I.R.A., who were on the hills near the house would ambush them. However, the soldiers never turned up in the end!!!

My Grandad remembers his dad - Samuel Sweetnam and his Grandfather - (Dont know his name) Sweetnam telling him stories about the Black and Tans and the IRA. Both would randomly barge in on any night and demand a meal and their best bed in the house for a night. They would also have them take them off to wher ever they needed to go in the horse and cart. In my great + great great grandad's case it would have been Skibbereen which was around seven miles from where they lived. But it could take much longer as lots of roads were 'cut', meaning either the Black and Tans or the IRA would blow up part of a road with gunpowder so you couldn't get through. So, it was very inconvenien But, if you didn't oblige, you would be shot

Naomi Sweetnam
Abbeystrewry National School, Skibbereen.

Lá amháin bhí mo sin-seanaithear ag dul isteach sa siopa agus chonaic sé an saighdiuirí rá le fear chun a mála linne le rudaí ón siopa uch duirt an fear ní raibh sé alhailte mar ní raibh alón airgid aige. Duirt an saighdiuirí dul isteach agus cheanaigh an rudaí mar chaithig tú airgead a th talhairt mar ní chaithig an saighdiuirí airgead a talhairt.

Clár Ní Ríordáin
Gaelscoil Dhroichead na Banndan.

The Blackened Hands used to barge in through the door and demand food from my great grandmother, kate Jennings.
She was from Roscarbery.
Whether she had enough for them or not, she had to supply them with food.
If she hadn't, they would shot her.

Amber Bryan
The Model School, Dunmanway.

1916 - 1923

FOOD NOW‼

Once my great great Granuncle and Aunt had to give food to British soldiers if they asked. You had to because they had guns. The British knew which houses to get food in. So, at the dead of night they would knock on the door and expect food.

Matthew Benn
Abbeystrewry National School, Skibbereen.

My Grandfather's Grandfather had a pub in North Street, Skibbereen at the time of the Revolution. One night British Soldiers "Black and Tans" were drinking there and got very agressive. MY great great grandfather refused them any more drinks, So one of the soldiers shot a bullet up through the ceiling with his rifle. There were family living upstairs, So my great great grandfather caught him and threw them all out by himself, they never came Back either. His name was Con Carey and his name is still over the same building today.

Yasmin Atalay
Scoil Naomh Bhríde, Union Hall.

In 1918-1919 the Black and Tans would come and check out the village. The local people didn't like the Black and Tans. They would quickly go into their homes or if they were in the village shopping, they would go home quickly. Michael's grandmother had a pub at the bottom of the village. The Black and Tans would go into the pub and demand whiskey. They wouldn't pay for it, they'd roll hand grenades around the floor of the pub to frighten everyone.

Joseph Mahon
Leap National School.

Rode horse into house

Ciara Dullea
Scoil Mhaoilíosa, Knockavilla.

One night there was a party in a house in Meenies lots of locals were there. Patrick Dullea was standing on the hill watching for the Brittish army. He saw them comming and mounted his horse. He galloped off to tell the people at the party house. He was in such a panic that he rode the horse right into the sitting room of the house

Judge 'sentenced' to hard labour

Lara O'Donovan,
St Joseph's GNS, Skibbereen.

During the War of Independence in 1921. The local R.M. "resident magistrate", Daniel O'Connell, lived at Killeena House, Cregh near Baltimore.

The local I.R.A kidnapped the Judge and burned down the house in Killeena.

His kidnappers, farmers from near Skeagh, took the prisoner with them to the local Creamery one morning. Daniel O'Connell gave out to his kidnappers when he saw women pulping beet at the ceamery (pulping beet is a very physical job). So after that he gave his kidnappers an idea.

For the remainder of the period of captivity the judge was brought to the creamery every day to pulp beet.

The R.M. when released never prosecutted his kidnappers or women

The End!

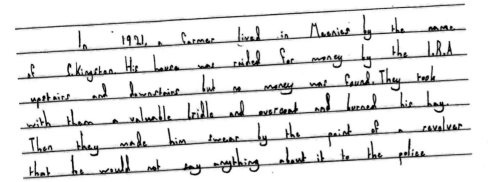

'In 1921, a farmer lived in Meenies by the name of Silkington. His house was raided for money by the IRA upstairs and downstairs but no money was found. They took with them a valuable bridle and overcoat and burned his hay. Then they made him swear by the point of a revolver that he would not say anything about it to the police.'

Vincent Keane
Drimoleague National School.

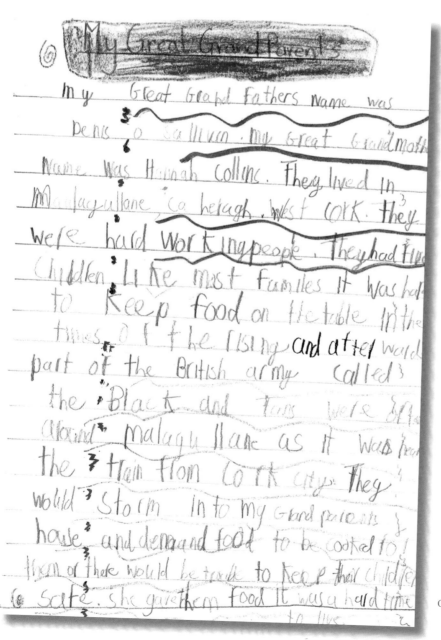

Neil O'Sullivan
Caheragh National School.

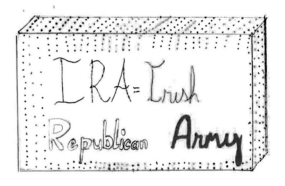

Kadi Deasy
Gaelscoil Mhichíl Uí Choileáin, Clonakilty.

A hard time to live

During the year of 1916 Mary Kate fell in love with English solider named Archie Perrier who was fighting with the Black and Tans and he was based in Kinsale. Mary Kate could not tell her parents about her relationship with this English solider as her father was a strong republican. Mary Kate loved her family and did not want to break her father's heart so she kept her relationship a secret. After the death of her parents Mary Kate married Archie in secret in Kinsale. They later moved to England where they lived very happy ever after.

Cian Ring
Gaelscoil Dhroichead na Banndan.

First cars in the area

122- When my Nan's father was going to school, he drove himself and his 3 sisters in a donkey and trap, (they lived in the townlands of Ballygurteen) there everyday. Sometimes, though, they had to turn around and trot back to the farm as quickly as they could, for there would be a deep trench dug across the lane and they didn't want to be caught in an ambush. The trench was dug by the I.R.B. because the was a van full of Black & Tans expected to pass by. One day, on their way to school, they heard an engine of a car on the road coming towards them. It was the doctor, with one of the first cars in the area! Now, the donkey didn't like the look of this 'four-legged', noisy thing. In fact the poor donkey was terrified! The donkey reared up, (trap and all!) brayed and jumped over the ditch!

Tara McCarthy
The Model School, Dunmanway.

Chapter 2

THE BLACK & TANS

The brutality of the Black and Tans is a recurring theme throughout
the collection, and the fear and terror they evoked in the Irish people
is still palpable today in these accounts.

The Black and Tans were very feared people. The police force were running low on people so they sent the Black and Tans in. They got their name because they had no proper uniform. They had to use the army pants (which was a tan colour) and a police jacket (which was a black colour). That's how they became known as the Black and Tans. They patrolled the country side using crossley tenders (like land rovers).

Ava Scarlett
Leap National School.

MY Great GrandMother
Annie Walsh 19 — 2011

Drunk and ruthless

'My great grandmother Annie Walsh was born in Clifton in 1915. She was just 6 years old when the Black and Tans were sent to Clifton. They arrived in Clifton by train on St Patrick's Day 1921. They were very drunk and ruthless men. They began burning houses and firing shots at people and houses. My great grandmother remembers being really frightened and her mother hid her and her siblings in the fireplace so they wouldn't get hurt by stray bullets or glass. They burned down 13 houses that night and killed two people.'

Alaia O'Sullivan
Caheragh National School.

At the bottom of Lahana Hill there is a derelict remains of a house. During the time of the revolution, the Black and Tans did a drive by shooting past this house. There were people inside of the house at the time. Afterwards the furniture and beds were riddled with bulletholes.

Emily Collins
Drimoleague National School.

Lyre shooting

There was a man named Larry Cunningham. During the civil war he went to see his family in Lyre. He was afraid the Black and Tan's would follow him so he slept in a bog. One night he went to the pub The Black and Tans followed him. They shot him through the window. They were about half a kilometer away.

'There was a man named Larry Cunningham. During the Civil War he went to see his family in Lyre. He was afraid the Black and Tans would follow him so he slept in a bog. One night he went to the pub the Black and Tans followed him. They shot him through the window. They were about a half a kilometre away.'

Gavin Nyhan
Kilcolman National School.

Gary Lordan
Kilcolman National School.

This would happen time to time and for revenge as they didn't get any information out of them, they were passing the road straight south from the dwelling house as it now stands and one of them "The Black And tans" fired a shot with a high powered rifle, piercing the glass in the window of the kitchin going through the glass and knocking down some of the plaster on the opposite wall of the house.
Today the sash of this window is still kept as a reminder of what the family went through during these troubled times.

Michael Collins
Drimoleague National School.

Maebh Doyle
Scoil Naomh Seosamh, Laragh.

My Great Granfather and my Great Gran uncle faught against the Black And Tans. There is a bullet fired from a Black And Tan gun lodged in the corner cupboard in the kitchen were my Grandparents live. This was meant for my Great Granfather. The bullet et Just missed my Great Gran mother while she sat on the old settle.

Natasha O'Donoghue
Drimoleague National School.

Mary Kate Falvey (nee Nyhan)
My Great Granny's sister.

One night the Black and Tans raided their house in Castletown Kennigh under Major Percival. Mary Kate pretended to have a turn and lied down on rifles and her sister was praying over her so that they wouldnot not look under her.

Major Percival threatened my Great Great granny Katherine Nyhan. He put his rifle to her chest to kill her but changed his mind and shot her pony instead.

Chloe Kelly
Scoil Eoin National School, Innishannon.

Black and Tan's

Áine O'Brien
Scoil Eoin National School, Innishannon.

My Mams Family

My Mam's Dads Donal Kelly's Uncle Timoithy Hourihan was shot by the black and tans in September 1920. He was minding his own business when bang shot, his wife found him dead, then later died of a broken heart.

Geraldine McCarthy
Coppeen National School.

My Great Grandmother and my Great Grandfather lived on a big dairy farm in Schull. They had many local men, working for them.

A lot of the workers were young and were members of the local I.R.A Organisation.

My Grandfather was well liked in Schull. He helped the poor and he employed many people, his family lived in the same house for generations.

He was Anglo Irish.

Life on the farm was very busy, One day my Great Grandmother was giving the work men, their dinner in the kitchen.

Suddenly, there was a bang at the front door. The work men ran out the back door. They knew it was the Black and Tans. They ran up to the orchard, and hid in the hay stacks. Meanwhile the Black and Tans forced their way into my Great Grandmother kitchen. They demanded to know where the men had gone.

She told them that they had gone out the back door. She was frightened.

The Black and Tans looked everywhere for the men but could not find them. The work men did not return to work on the farm ever again.

Beatrice Attridge
Abbeystrewry National School, Skibbereen.

Our grandad told us that the black and tans or even the free staters would go into a barn and stab the hay with pikes to see if anyone was hiding underneath it and if they were they would probably been killed. Most republicans had a secret door under the hay so people would be able to hide without being killed.

Lilly Heaton-Jones & Jessie Holmes
St Joseph's GNS, Skibbereen.

I went to my grandaunt Lydia Sweetnam to get my stories. She lives in Clohane, Skibbreen.

She told me that my great- grandfather, Thomas Sweetnam used go to a wooded area about quarter of a mile from his house if he thought he was in danger from Black and Tans. He owned a big farm and house which made him a target. They would not shoot the women or children only the men. At night he would go in the wooded area near a waterfall where he could see his house and farm in the distance. He slept there as it was too dangerous to go home. In the morning if he saw it was safe, he would go home. He lived in fear.

Gavin Sweetnam
Abbeystrewry National School, Skibbereen.

Hide by a tree

'It was the winter of 1921 when the Black and Tans started arriving at my great grandfather's house … They came a few nights every week … When they came late in the evening he would hide by a tree in a field behind the house. They searched the house and shed but never found him.'

Jack Grace
St Patrick's Boys National School

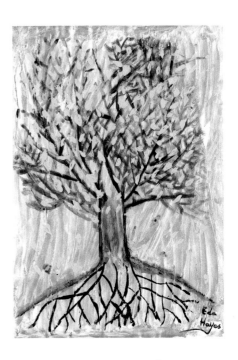

Ída Ní Aodha
Gaelscoil Dhroichead na Banndan.

Sleep in the barn

Amber Bryan
The Model School, Dunmanway.

Kate's husband, John, used to sleep in the barn for fear that when The Blackened Hands came in, they'd shoot him.

John and Kate's children weren't allowed to talk to anyone at home about all that happened at home in case the talk spread and the Blackened Hands heard of it.

Crash, Bang, Wallop!

My Great Grandfather, John Jennings, used to watch out of the window to see if the Blackened Hands were coming.

One time, he was perched on something (probably a stool) and he fell off!

Thankfully, the Blackened Hands weren't there!

Amber Bryan,
Lisbealad,
Dunmanway.

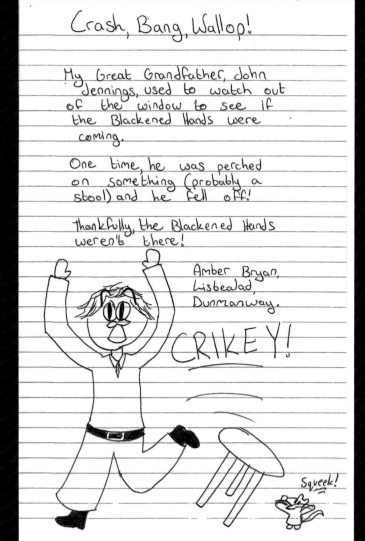

CRIKEY!

Squeek!

Amber Bryan
The Model School, Dunmanway

Strained eyes

Our grandad

Vin O'Mahony is 91 and is from Coolodreen in Leap. His Aunty Briggy needed glasses from a young age. They used to say that her eyesight was strained looking out for the black and tans. Her house was a safe house. The lookout was in the corn shed. They used to hide the Irish Rebels up stairs in their attic.

Uinseann O'Mahony
Lisavaird National School.

David O'Mahoney was tipped off that he was to be targeted by the Black and Tans. He stayed up for nights on end waiting for them. He never told his wife or children. One night the Black and Tans came and poured petrol around the outside of their shop and house and lit it on fire. A side door was missed and they escaped up Warners Lane. They stayed with their neighbours, the O'Learys, for the night. They lost everything in the fire. The only thing David brought with him were the shop ledgers. The next morning when they went back they found that the only thing that survived was Margaret's silver thimble.

After the fire all the children split apart and moved into different relations' houses. For years they all lived apart. Eventually they were able to rent a house in Main Street, Bantry. They moved again to Rock Villas in Bantry after a few years. They never recovered financially from the fire.

Some time later Jim, David's son, was teaching in North Cork and was shot. He later died of his wounds. His brother Pat went to America and never returned.

Sive Buckley
The Model School, Dunmanway.

'General Percival who was the commander of the British soldiers during the troubles, came to the house and ordered them to leave so that he could burn the house. Dr Dorothy Stopford Price was treating the grandfather who was on his deathbed upstairs. She angrily told Colonel Percival that he should leave the house immediately as there was a dying man there. The General left in disgust. Dr Price was the only woman to stand up to General Percival'.

Jason O'Shea
Reenascreena National School.

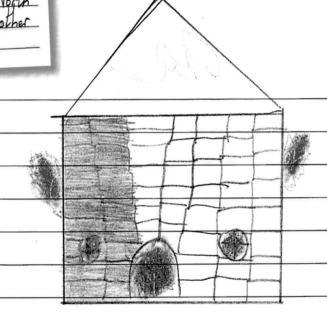

Connor Crowley
St Joseph's National School, Dromore.

Neilus Connolly is my great-great-grandfather. He lived in Coolnagrane, but his house was burnt down by the Black in Tans in 1918, because Neilus was a wanted man and the Black in Tans hoped he would run out of the house.

Rebecca Connolly
St Joseph's GNS, Skibbereen.

Terrible effect

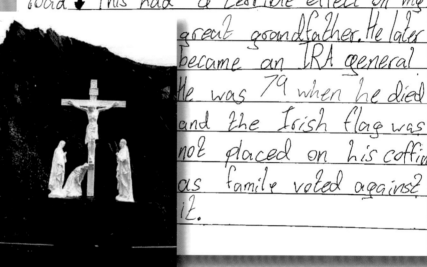

Tadgh O Flaherty
Down in Kerry, in an IRA hideout, Tadgh my great grandfather was just a little boy. He was sitting on the lap of a freedom fighter, when suddenly a group of Black and Tans broke in and kidnapped the freedom fighter. They took him to Dingle, where they tied him to the back of a truck. Where he died there is a cross on the side of the road ↓ This had a terrible effect on my great grandfather. He later became an IRA general. He was 79 when he died and the Irish flag was not placed on his coffin as famile voted against it.

Lachlan O'Regan
Rathmore National School.

Screaming in pain

During the war of independence the Black and Tans captured a local man from Spiddal in County Galway who was in the local flying column of the Old IRA. They wanted him to tell them where his comrades were but he refused so they dragged him across a huge sharp rock. This was particularly painful because they had stripped him of his clothes. Local people could hear him screaming in pain but he didn't betray his friends. The locals named the rock Leac an tóinacháin after that, which roughly translates as 'the arse dragging rock'.

Lara Nic Suibhne
Gaelscoil Dhochtúir Uí Shúilleabháin, An Sciobairín.

Matt kiely was a brother of P.K. He was taken hostage in Dungarvan by the Black and Tans. When the Black and Tans were going around in their vehicles they used Matt kiely as a human shield to stop people shooting

at them as they drove around the town Matt kiely was never shot but he suffered psychological trauma following on from this treatment from the Black and Tans.

Rachael Gaffney
Scoil Naomh Seosamh, Laragh.

'Tan mentally affected

On one occasion my great grandfather was in the house with his father as the rest of the family had gone to a funeral, when one of the Black & Tan soldiers arrived in brandishing a revolver. This Tan was mentally affected as a result of his involvement in World War 1. At an earlier date, my great-great grandfather had a verbal run in with this soldier when he came to take away some hen eggs and he told my great grandfather that he had come to shoot him. He caught my great grandfather by the shoulder and had the gun pointed at him. He then told him to run away as fast as he could. My great grandfather was lucky he did not panic and run as they had orders to shoot anyone running from them trying to escape. When he did not run, the Tan then shot between his legs and the bullet was found imbedded between flagstones in the house at a later date.

Finn O'Mahony
Scoil na mBuachaillí, Clonakilty.

They started to search the small cottage. Queenie was asleep in her little bed. Without hesitation the soldiers pulled Queenie out of her bed thinking that someone could be hiding underneath it. When Queenie was woken, she began to scream at the top of her voice!! The soldiers were embarrassed and stressed with the little girl screaming hysterically, and they abandoned the search. The soldiers left the house to everyones joy and relief. Sadly, Sonny was captured the following year and interned.

Ava Scarlett
Leap National School.™

One day that farm worker went onto' the country road and buried a tin bucket in the middle of the road with only the bottom rim showing. A truck load of Black and Tans were passing they saw what they thought was a coal mine but it was actually the bucket. They spent hours on end shooting at it until they discovered it was a hoax.

Kate Coppinger
St Joseph's GNS, Skibbereen.

WIRE ROPE

Jack & Tadg Crowley
Dreeny National School.

Tadgh O' Driscoll from Rabbit Island off Union Hall used to row in from the Island to the mainland to take part in ambushes on the Tans. He tied a wire rope between two trees, the lorries hit the wire, lost control and the lorries drove into the lake.

The Day My Great Grandad Saved
The IRA From The Black & Tans

My Great Grandad's name was Jeremiah O'Donovan. He was a Publican and a Farmer and lived at Fishers Cross, Castlefreke, Clonakilty. He got married to Bridget O'Mahony in 1916.

In 1921 the Black and Tans came into the Bar, looking for the road to Rathbarry. My Great Grandad showed them the road (which was the long route). They had a drink in the Bar and went on their way on foot.

As soon as the Black and Tans were out of sight. My Great Grandad saddled his horse and rode to Rathbarry using a different road – a shorter route to the one he showed the Black and Tans. The IRA were hiding out in Rathbarry. Jeremiah alerted the IRA that the Black and Tans were coming and by the time they arrived in Rathbarry, the IRA were long gone, thanks to my Great Grandad – Jeremiah O'Donovan.

Cathal O'Donovan
S.N Rath A' Bharraigh/Rathbarry National School.

The stolen cob

The Story of the Stolen cob

I heard this story from my great-grandmother who is now 96 years old and in Skibbereen Hospital She told me, that my great-great grandfather, George Whitley, lived in Skeagh Schull during those years and he told her how the black and tans (british auxilary army) came one evening and demanded his cob (small hourse/pony) You dare not refuse.

My great-great grandfather thought he'd never again see his cob. To his delight three days later the cob was returned unharmed. At that time travel on horsebac may have been the only means of transport.

Chloe Ronan
St Mary's Primary School, Rosscarbery.

Left quiet

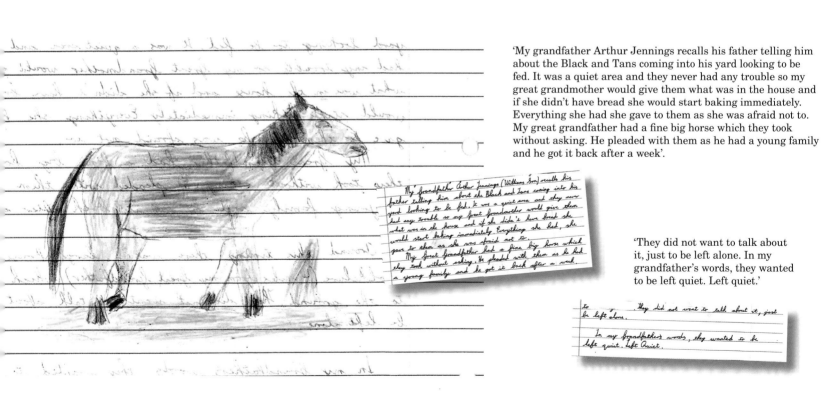

'My grandfather Arthur Jennings recalls his father telling him about the Black and Tans coming into his yard looking to be fed. It was a quiet area and they never had any trouble so my great grandmother would give them what was in the house and if she didn't have bread she would start baking immediately. Everything she had she gave to them as she was afraid not to. My great grandfather had a fine big horse which they took without asking. He pleaded with them as he had a young family and he got it back after a week'.

'They did not want to talk about it, just to be left alone. In my grandfather's words, they wanted to be left quiet. Left quiet.'

Killian Kingston
The Model School, Dunmanway.

My nan Mary Dwyer lived in the Skeames Island. It was she told me of the dissiculties they had in those days. Her mother had told her that the Black and Tans went into the islands searching for the free staters. The free staters were on the run from the Black and Tans.

They went from one island to the next with rifles and bayonettes. They had to cook and feed the Black and Tans and the free staters too with the very little food they had.

The Islanders osten gave up their beds to the Black and Tans who were osten covered in fleas and lice as they slept in outhouses and hen houses. The Black and Tans set fire to houses in Castleisland.

The women on the island were afra and frightened as their men used to be away fishing for weeks on end, fishing for lobsters along the coast. This lest the women vulnerable.

The free staters used to bury their guns at the top of the strands at the high water marks and return later on to retrieve them.

Lydia Dwyer
Lisheen National School.

When the Black and Tans came into the islands they used to sink their punts so that the free staters couldn't escap Nan's grandfather was away fishing off Kinsale at this time, and his boat was saved.

The free staters went from the Skeame island to Horse island where they hid in the copper mines.

'During the 2 or 3 nights that the Black and Tans stayed there, my great grandparents either had to sleep on the floor or stay up all night. Also they had to kill their chickens and pluck the feathers off them to feed all the hungry men. There was no food left in the house by the time the men had left … The people in the house also had to obey everything the Black and Tans said or else they would have been tortured or killed. Before they had left, a lot of the houses around the area would have been burned.'

Kyle O'Sullivan
Lisheen National School.

During the two or three nights that the Black and Tans stayed there my great grandparents either had to sleep on the floor or some stayed up all night. Also they had to kill their chickens and pluck the feathers off them to feed all the hungry men. There was no food lest in the house by the time the men had lest all of it. The people in the house also had to obey everything the Black and Tans said or else they would have been tortured or killed. Before they had lest, a lot of the houses around this area would have been burned

Died of shock

In the early 1920s my great gran uncle got raided by the black and tans many times. My great gran uncle's name was Mr Michale John Kingston. After all the raiding my gran moth Mini Kingston died from the shock.

'In the early 1920s my great great granduncle got raided by the Black and Tans many times. My great great granuncle's name was Mr Michael John Kingston. After all the raiding my [great, great] grandmother Mini Kingston died from the shock.'

Nicholas Deane
Kilgarriffe National School.

Don't come back

P.K. is the man in the middle of the photograph
He is my great grandfather
(my dad's mum's dad)

William Hill was a member of the Black and Tans around Cork in the 1920s. He was injured while carrying out some of the Black and Tans operations. He was brought to the South Infirmary Hospital and was seen by P.K. who was a young doctor at the time. He made a full recovery. When he was recovered he asked P.K. "What will I do now?" P.K. answered "Go down to the Inis fallen and don't ever come back again". Many years later P.K. went to a race meeting in the U.K. While he was walking around the races a man stepped down from one of the bookies boxes and said "Here's the man who saved my life". It turned out that the bookies was William Hill who was the proprietor of a well known bookemaker business, which is still in operation today.

Rachael Gaffney
Scoil Naomh Seosamh, Laragh.

'Tans & cows

My great gran father John o leary from toames Macroom said he would have to be very careful when bringing in his cows for milking as the black and tans could be hiding between and also they used to cut the cows tails off.

Sarah Whitehead
Derrinacahara National School

Jack remembered being sick in bed as a child with the measles and the Tans coming in and pulling him out of bed to search under the mattress. He remembered his uncle Michael Keenan, from Glandore who was staying with them at the time, and who was also a member of the I.R.A., being put up against the front door with John McCarthy with the Tans threatening to shoot them both until his mother, Kathleen, who was pregnant at the time, came out and stood in front of both of them and told the Tans they would have to shoot her first. They relented but took Michael Keenan away to Cork Jail where they kept himself and John L. O'Sullivan in a cage inside the main gate to humiliate them in the hope of getting information out of them

Liadhain Ní hÓgáin
Scoil Naomh Bhríde, Union Hall.

This is a picture of John McCarthy and his wife Kathleen in later years taken outside the door where once she bravely stood in front of her husband and brother when the Tans threatened to shoot them.

Greg Mulhall
St Joseph's National School, Dromore.

Jack recalled Rosscarbery as being 'a very hot spot during the troubles mainly because there was a military barrack there and regular British troops and R.I.C. occupied it. The Auxiliaries (see note at end) and the Tans also occupied the courthouse in Newtown, near where he lived. The I.R.A. were also busy there and regularly attacked the British forces. The British were at one stage so afraid to venture out into the countryside that they would tie the Fehily brothers, Jerh and Paddy, who were prisoners at the time, up in front of their truck. They knew this would prevent the I.R.A. from ambushing them for fear of shooting the Fehilys'. He remembered the Black & Tans times of curfew and the fact that people had even to have their names on the carts going to creamery or town and would be prosecuted if they did not obey this. He also remembered the night Rosscarbery R.I.C. Barracks was taken by the West Cork Brigade under General Tom Barry on the 30th March, 1921.

Liadhain Ní hÓgáin
Scoil Naomh Bhríde, Union Hall.

My Great Great grandfather - John McCarthy

A miracle

One day in 1921 the Black and Tans burst in to the house and started shooting like crazy. They kept firing shots up the stairs at a statue of our Lady. The shots went all around the statue but not one bullet hit our lady.

The family and our great, great-great grand aunt Nan were extremely traumatised and greatful to escape unharmed, they felt that the statue remaining untouched was a miracle!

Donal and Caitriona O'Neill
Caheragh National School.

When the family returned to the house they found that it had not burned down and it still there across from the school. The flames had only reached the heart of the Sacret Heart picture. This was regarded on a Miracle in the locality and for many years often people came to see this picture which is now in Pride of Place in Nualaï Home in Dalkey.

Eve Murphy & Orlagh McBride
Dromleigh National School.

Ghost story

Colm Harrington
Rathmore National School.

There once was a Corporal heading from Schull to Dunmanway. He rode on horse back and he was a Black and Tan. As he rode through Glounaphooca bog, the wind arose a massive wave in a flat, lifeless lake nestled between two peat banks.

They say the Corporal thought it was a beautiful white horse and so he chased it, fell into the lake and drowned. The next day the English Army came looking for the Corporal. They found his body on the bank of the lake.

They say you can still see his ghost riding across the lake to this day!

ROLE AS A SCOUT

Greg Mulhall
St Joseph's National School, Dromore.

His role as a scout was to keep a close eye on any Black+Tans in the Bantry and Muintir Bháire area. When he spotted Black and Tans he would report it to the Durrus IRA. He was only 15 years old when he done this. He also got a medal for this. It is a very nice big medal in my opinion.

Tree....

In the IRA at 16

My great granuncle Patrick O'Donovan was brought into the IRA at the age of sixteen! He grew up in Arrighan. He was in the march in Dublin. He also fought but he did not like it and got arrested.

Jack Hennigan
Ballinacarriga National School.

My name is John Murray, I was born in 1902. I live in a rural West Cork. I have one older sister, our father died of pneumonia when I was just a baby, so life was not always easy growing up. I went to Derrinacahera school but because there was so much work to do at home on the farm, I left school at age 11. But a lot of my friends at school, also left when they were young, it was normal at the time. I worked on the farm every day to help my family. It was hard work. When I was 16 I joined the I.R.A.

The type of jobs I had to do as a member of the IRA.....

- Scouting – That is being on look out in case the black and tans were coming. Scouting was also called centuring. We would be allowed carry a gun, especially when we were scouting. We had very little arms in our branch. We had mainly shotguns which were not as good as riffles. Sometimes the IRA would raid the local RIC (Royal Irish Constabulary) barracks to get riffles. They were the guards of the Country at the time. I heard a story about another branch of the IRA who raided a navy ship at Bantry Bay and I heard a lot of riffles were stolen from them then.

- Blocking roads/cutting roads/breaking bridges/knocking trees – we would have to block the roads so the black and tans couldn't travel on them. Local people, like us would know all the detours or we would travel through the field. It was very hard work to block roads, our tools were very basic, we used pic axes, cross cut saws, sledges and crowbars. I remember hearing about a story that happened in Dunmanway town, when the IRA shot a horse at the bottom of Castle St. So the horse and cart would block the road and a horse would not be easy to move if the black and tans tried to follow the IFA people

Alice O'Donovan |
Togher National School. |

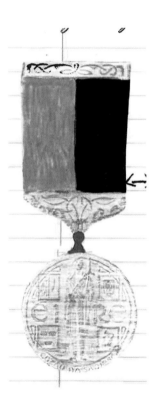

Aislinn O'Riordan |
Scoil Naomh Seosamh, Laragh. |

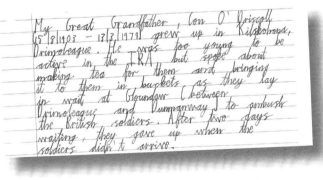

'My great grandfather, Con O'Driscoll … was too young to be active in the IRA but spoke about making tea for them and bringing it to them in buckets as they lay in wait … to ambush the British soldiers.'

Eoin O'Sullivan |
St Patrick's BNS, Skibbereen. |

'My great grandmother was Kitty O'Brien. She lived with her aunt as her mother was very sick. She loved to play with her dog as well.

One day she decided to stay at home and help her aunt with the daily chores .... Their neighbour, a man by the name of N. Hagerty was on the run from the Black and Tans. He rushed through the door and Kitty's aunt told him to hide under Kitty's bed. Kitty was instructed to get into the bed.

When the Black and Tans came following a little while later, Kitty's aunt told them that there was only a sick child up in bed. The Black and Tans marched up the stairs and when they landed in her bedroom all they saw was the little girl Kitty in her bed'.

| Emily Dullea
| Drimoleague National School

Rebel under her toes

This is a story about Paul's grandmother Charlotte. She was fourteen years old and lived with her mother in Dublin.

Late one night, her mother came into her room and said, "Quick, quick." Charlotte went into her mother's bed and was just falling asleep when she felt something under her toes. It was a rebel.

| Lucija Kluzniak Madajczak
| Abbeystrewry National School, Skibbereen.

Said Ernie o' Malley of Jim gorman, " [Jim] had blue eyes glinting out of a tanned face. He was an Irish-Australian. He had fought through the Great war and was a Crack shot. He had assurance and could curse better than any man on the hills "

One day the Free Staters paid a 'visit' to Jim and Rebecca in their Cappawhite home. It was very unexpected so When they burst in the door, Jim had to think on his feet. They came into the house and asked him; "Are there any men in the house?" Suddenly Jim had an idea. "Yes" he said "Upstairs in the bedroom."

The free Staters charged upstairs and went in. To their astonishment, they saw Rebecca in bed, with a newborn baby boy. The Free Staters went away, leaving Jim with a cross Rebecca who needless to remark, was not too pleased with Jim's Idea of a joke!

Another time, the British came looking for Jim and his friends. They were hiding upstairs But when the Brits came in the door, Rebecca was so cross about them disturbing their baby, she marched them all out of the house! Jim was so relieved, they had a party! (they did live in a pub! after all.)

Eveanna Goulding
Scoil Bhríde National School, Ballydehob.

Fastnet raid

The Fastnet Raid

In June 1921 the Fastnet Lighthouse was raided by the Irish Republican Army. During the war of independence the English hid ammunition in lighthouses. Generally people raided lighthouses that were easily accessible from land however more powerful ammunition in further away lighthouses. The IRA waited for a calm night to raid the lighthouse. Six or seven men went out to the lighthouse and attached a few men to ropes and pulled them up on to the rock. Supposedly the men were after the explosives used to power the foghorn. The keepers never locked the doors of the fastnet as they never expected any intruders. They held all of the keepers hostage and stole what they could. They ended up with seventeen boxes of gun cotton and three boxes of detonators and primers were all loaded on to their boat the "Marie Cait". All of the spoils weighed around one ton. The men accomplished an impossible task.

'In June 1921 the Fastnet Lighthouse was raided by the Irish Republican Army. During the War of Independence the English hid ammunition in lighthouses. Generally people raided lighthouses that were easily accessible from land, however, more powerful ammunition was in further away lighthouses. The IRA waited for a calm night to raid the lighthouse. Six or seven men went out to the lighthouse and attached a few men to ropes and pulled them up onto the rock. Supposedly the men were after the explosives used to power the foghorn. The keepers never locked the doors of the Fastnet as they never expected any intruders. They held all of the keepers hostage and stole what they could. They ended up with seventeen boxes of gun cotton, and three boxes of detonators and primers were all loaded onto their boat the "Marie Cait". All of the spoils weighted about one ton. The men accomplished an impossible task.'

Ellen O'Donovan
Scoil Bhríde National School, Ballydehob.

They then rowed back. That night they stored the explosives in one of their own houses. The next night they went out to a field and dug a hole in my dads field now. They buried all the explosives that they got in the 'Fastnet.' I asked my dad If the explosives are still in our field but he said they dug out after a while and took them.

Liadh O'Donovan
Scoil Mhuire National School, Schull.

My Great Grandfather Patrick was involved in blowing up a bridge near the town of Skibbereen. The Bridge was located at Lisanohig about 3 miles from the town. The local volunteer Companies decided to take down bridges to prevent the RIC and British Army soldiers from moving freely in and out areas where they knew, that men were on the run. This allowed these men get away without being captured. Patrick was injured by doing so and suffered from a bad back for the rest of his life. He died on March the 27th, 1961 and is buried in Drinagh graveyard.

Ellie Curtin |
St Mary's Primary School, Rosscarbery. |

The bomb escapade

There was a sergeant and fourteen police men in the Barrack in Drimoleague. The IRA decided to attak it one night. They had a bomb. They placed it at the door of the Barrack.

Michael Collins |
Drimoleague National School. |

Their mission was to break in and get the guns which were stored there and belonged to the police. But the bomb instead of blowing in the door it blew it out across the road to what is now Beamishe's Corn Mill or Centra's shop.
It broke all the windows in the Mill along with damaging the walls.
It was said at the time that the owner of the mill, Mr. T.J Beamish, he drew hugh compensation off the British establishment for the damage done to the Mill. He was the only one that gained out of the bomb escapade

There used to be a cattle fair in Skibbereen in the month of May. Farmers from Leap, Drinagh, Union Hall and all the neighbouring parishes would walk their cattle to the fair. Donal's father and grandfather had cattle for the fair. They had got up early to set off when word came not to go by Connonagh as "the place was all smoke". Instead they used another route to get to Skibbereen. A house in Connonagh was burnt to the ground and that was what caused all the smoke. John Barry who was principal teacher in the Mall School lived in that house with his two unmarried sisters. He was also an intelligence officer and collected stories for the I.R.A. He had also donated money to the I.R.A. John Barry had red hair but he dyed it black when he was on the run. He wasn't at home. Shortly before the house was burned, John's two sisters were ordered to dress warmly and

Ava Scarlett
Leap National School.

get out of the house. The house was sprinkled with petrol and burnt to the ground.

Howe Strand Coastguard Station

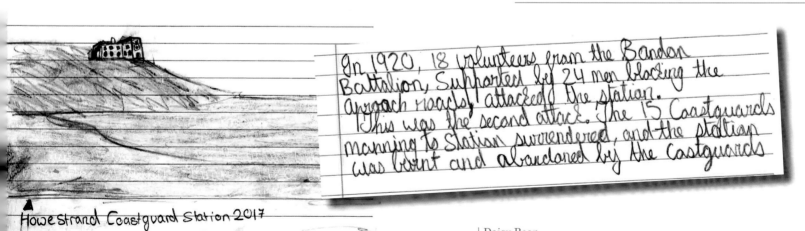

Howe Strand Coastguard Station 2017

In 1920, 18 volunteers from the Bandon Battalion, supported by 24 men blocking the approach roads, attacked the station. This was the second attack. The 15 Coastguards manning the station surrendered, and the station was burnt and abandoned by the Coastguards

Daisy Bean
Gaelscoil Dhroichead na Banndan.

'In 1921 Lord Bandon was kidnapped and held hostage for three weeks. The man who was given the job of guarding him was Dan Leabhair O'Leary … The IRA threatened to execute Lord Bandon if the British went ahead with executing IRA prisoners. It is said that Leabhair and the Lord got on very well. In the evening they played cards and drank beer, probably Clonakilty Wrestler. Leabhair often rode horseback to Slatterys pub in Ahiohill to purchase flagons of beer to bring back to him and his prisoner. The Lord was released after three weeks unharmed. Dan O'Leary was an interesting, witty local character. He was nicknamed Leabhair because he was well read.'

Milo Forsey
Kilcolman National School.

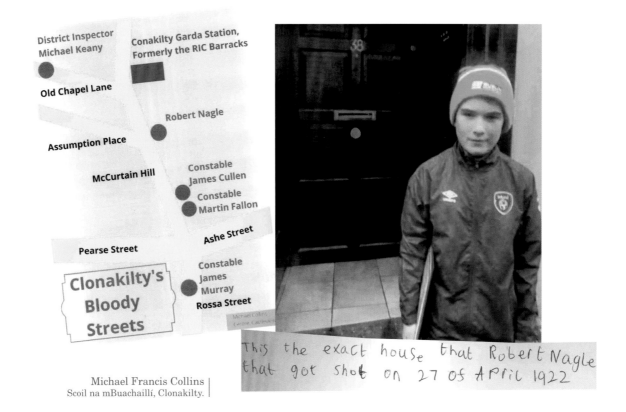

Michael Francis Collins
Scoil na mBuachaillí, Clonakilty.

This the exact house that Robert Nagle that got shot on 27 05 April 1922

The Schull Bank Robbery

Ellen O'Donovan
Scoil Bhríde National School, Ballyde[...]

On Holy Thursday of June 1921 money was being transported from Schull to Ballydehob for the fair when it was stolen by local men who stole it thinking that the Irish Republican Army (IRA) would be blamed. They stole the money and hid in a clearing along Schull road. The robbers then decided to continue along to Ballabán. Along the road they were caught trying to jump over a river by a woman named Nora Leahy (my great-grandmother). The ringleader was Callaghan and there were three other acomplices who still haven't been named to this day. After they were arrested they were tried in a Sinn Fein court made of Seán Lehane, Seán O'Driscoll, Seán McCarthy, Jim Hayes and Charlie Cotter. Around 500 pounds in cash was stolen and three of the robbers were setenced to deportation ordered to leave Ireland within a few months however the truce came a month later so the men no longer had to leave. The other robber was fined 50 pounds. To try and find the money they tied Callaghan to a rope and tried to threaten him by dangling him over a cliff to which Callaghan said "you won't cut it because then you'll never find the money". The money was later recovered.

Hazel Deane
Abbeystrewry National School, Skibbereen.

A man had a good big farm and a few guys pretended to be in the IRA. They evicted the man and took his farm. The real IRA and told them. One of the men went up to the farm and told the lads they had three minutes to get out or they would be shot. He said he knew the guys and if they touched the man he would take them out one by one

Sinn Féin Courts

The Sinn Fein Courts sometimes known as arbitration courts were formed and established in Ireland in 1917 and 1918. At the time the IRA were making the decisions. Judges were picked by the local IRA and women could also be chosen as judges. The Courts dealt with civil disputes such as trespassing, fighting and debts owed. The maximum fine was £10

John William Crowley was elected as a parish judge in the Sinn Fein Courts for the parish of Kilmacabea and Glandore The people chosen "were local men living and earing their bread within the area of their jurisdiction". They were "at risk by their judgements of mortally offending" because they knew the people who would be going to court- they were their neighbours. They were not paid for the job.

The British took over the Sinn Féin Courts in 1920 and started to prevent them from sitting. The British started to raid people's houses.

John recalls that one night four British soldiers came to Cappanaboha to raid the Crowley house. Inside, the judge was sitting at the table mending shoes. He had white hair and he was dressed in old clothes. The British didn't realise it was John William Crowley because they thought a judge would be wearing a suit. There was a hole in the wooden table and the solider sat at the table while he was questioning John William. He put his revolver into the hole and was swirling it around while he was waiting for John William to answer. He never copped on that the old man was in fact the judge and so John William had a lucky escape on that occasion.

John and his son Thomas were wanted by the Black and Tans so they often ran up to the hills and slept in ditches in the cold and rain. His wife and younger son went to live in safety with her relatives.

Mark Cooke
Leap National School.

Judge John William Crowley's house (1938)
Thomas and his wife Kathy.
Thomas was born in 1906 and was 14 when he was sleeping in the hills whilst hiding from The Tans ..

photo - courtesy of Maureen Crowle
Cappanaboha, Leap.

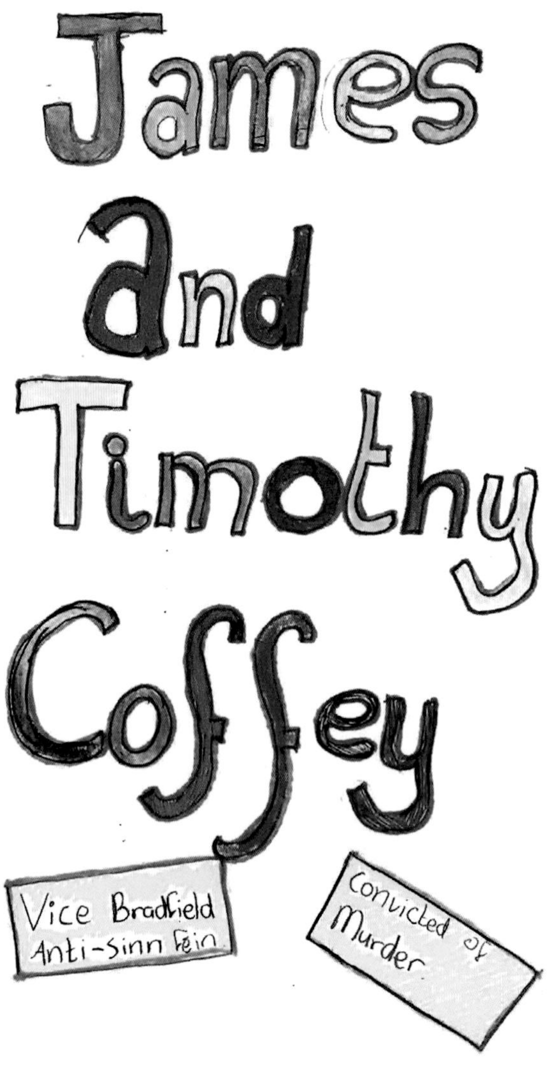

James and Timothy Coffey

Vice Bradfield
Anti-Sinn Féin

Convicted of Murder

.The brothers were taken from their father's house at night and shot dead at Kilrush near Enniskeane on the 14th of Febuary 1921.The head was nearly shot off one of them and the other was shot in the neck. On a card on one body was written "Vice Bradfield. Anti-Sinn Fein." On the other was written "Convicted of Murder." These killings appear to have been reprisal for the execution of Thomas Bradfield of Knockmacool as a suspected spy by the I.R.A. Both James and Timothey Coffey were burried in Abiohill graveyard.

Emma Galvin
Kilcolman National School.

Taken out and shot

I live in Derreennatra, Schull. Just over the road from my house is an old creamery. It is closed down now but people live in the house attached to it. Before the creamery was built there was just a dwelling house there. There is a story that there was a court held in that house and a man was taken out and shot after the court.

Conor Coughlan
Scoil Bhríde National School, Ballydehob.

In my pop's home town of Cahir, Co. Tipperary, there was a man named Potter who was an inspector in town. In later life, my Grandfather bought the house from his family.

It so happened that the British garrison captured a group of IRA soldiers with one of them being very important.
So the IRA captured Mr Potter and exchanged Mr Potter for the captured comrades.
The British would not release them and the I.R.A. felt they had no choice and took Mr Potter up the Vee in the comeragh mountains and executed him.
The towns people were very sad as Mr Potter was a civilian, even though he was employed by the British.
The story goes that the IRA. felt they had no choice as it was war and they felt they would lose face.

Michael Kennedy
Ballinadee National School.

Killing the RIC sergeant

Micheal Kilroy

'My great great grandfather Michael Kilroy was an Irish Republican Army officer during the war of Independence … Michael Kilroy and his men were attempting to set up an ambush on the Westport to Castlebar road on May 6th 1921 when 2 of their men were killed and 2 others were captured. The ambush had to be called off. Michael Collins in West Cork and the people in the Dublin headquarters wanted attacks and ambushes all over the country of Ireland, so Michael Kilroy was not going to give up. Two weeks later, Kilroy and his flying column were ready to try again. They changed the location to between Westport and Newport. In this attack, they managed to kill the RIC sergeant in Newport. This occurred near Michael Kilroy's home and the Black and Tans burned it down the following morning.'

Aisling O'Mahony
St Joseph's Girls National School, Clonakilty.

The Killing of Paddy O'Sullivan (Paddy Fly)

Paddy O'Sullivan, known as Paddy Fly, was a member of the Bauravilla Cumann of the IRA. He worked as a water diviner, sinking pumps, etc. He was a friendly man, a bit of a talker, who liked bowling and playing cards.

Members of the Bauravilla Cumann suspected him of passing on information to the RIC and wanted to 'get rid of him'. No-on had the courage to do the job because he was a nice, friendly person. So they sent him down to Mick O'Donovan and the Leap Cumann of the IRA, who had a reputation for being blood thirsty and gun happy.

They didn't shoot him straight away, they held him in custody. They brought him up to Keamore. They then brought Fr. Holland, a priest from Leap, up to Keamore at gun-point to give O'Sullivan the Last Rites. They stood him up on a ditch, shot up into the air at him with a revolver and afterwards knocked a ditch down on top of him and left him to the wildlife. (No trace of bones or skull was ever found at that spot when there was digging works there years later).

The shooter, Stephen Holland, went to the US with his girlfriend and never came back. Many other IRA members went to the US, including Patrick John Crisby, Coornishal. They stayed away, at least till things quietened down and some never came back. The IRA were very brutal. The least people deserved was a fair trial but Paddy Fly didn't get one.

rmaic
túir Uí Shúilleabháin, An Sciobairín.

Execution of the spy

Flor the fly was from Ballydehob. The IRA had warned him several times about giving information about to the R.I.C. but he wouldn't stop. He was tried and found guilty by the Military Court. Four men came to Crowley's house to shoot the spy. They were each given a rifle. Two were live- they had ammunition in them and the other two guns were dummies. Flor was marched up to Keamore and shot dead. His body was covered over and left there. It was never buried.

Mark Cooke
Leap National School

He was a very sociable man who would talk to anyone, on both sides. The local IRA thought he was unreliable. The Leap area wanted to "get rid of him".

The Leap IRA was very ruthless. The night before he was killed, he was brought to a house (which is near Frenches). Mrs. O Donovan lived in the house that he was brought to. Two men were chained to John. Mrs. O. Donovan had to feed him

The following morning, he was taken to a field in Cappanaloha. Fr. Holland (the parish priest at the time) was brought to him at gunpoint to give Paddy Fly his last rites. Then, Paddy was taken a few fields away and shot. Instead of burying him, he was left there and the ditch was knocked down to cover him. His body was never found! So Paddy was shot just for being kind to people!

During this time the Irish government set up Dail Eireann with their own courts. My great great granfather Jerry Con O Donovan (1868 to 1954) was a magristrate for the parish of Drimoleague

Usually 'informers' if caught would be executed. In one case since the informer had a large family another punishment was decided. He was made to take off all his clothes and run through a large "brake" of (furze) gorse

On February 7th 1921 my dads granny who was about 7 years old, was on holidays at her aunts house at Mohonagh, Skibbereen, when the news came through that her first cousin, Patrick O'Driscoll, aged 24 years was shot dead accidentally by one of his fellow soldiers in the old I.R.A while out on patrol. He was brought home to the house late that night and it was decided to bury him secretly in Aughadown graveyard to avoid trouble from the Black and Tans who were stationed in the Townhall in Skibbereen at that time. During the night the Black and Tans got the news from an informer of Patrick's death and raided the house in search of him. In the dark of night they turned everyone including eight young children out of the house. The children were frightened and cryied and then heard a gun shoot. While the soldiers were Ram sacking the house, one of them got accidently shot while looking up the chimney for guns.

Abbey Caverly
Kilcoe National School.

In 1922 Patrick O'Driscoll's body was exhumed from Aughadown Graveyard and taken to Kilcoe Church where mass was said. He was then reburied in the family plot in the Abbey Graveyard near Skibbereen. The funeral was led by the Brigade band from Bantry where shots were fired over his grave. All the shops were closed on that day as a mark of respect!

Bláthín Barry
Lisheen National School.

TIMOTHY WHOOLEYS ACCIDENTAL DEATH

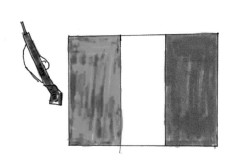

'Timothy Whooley, a member of the second or Clonakilty Battalion of the West Cork Brigade was on duty at Shannon Vale cross on the Bandon road. He was armed with a Peter the Painter (a type of gun), which he placed on the ground. The gun was picked up by one of his colleagues who knew little of the intricacies of the gun and before anyone could realise what was happening, Timothy Whooley was shot through the head and died almost immediately'

William Kingston
Kilgarriffe National School.

My Grandad told me a story about a boy called Patrick O'Mahony who found a gun in Cashel woods, sometime after the 1916 rising. His friend Jackie Jennings was messing with the gun and shot himself in the chin and died, this was a tragic story in the area at the time.

Conor and Liam Dooley
Lisavaird National School.

The man who got shot and killed by a child during the rising.

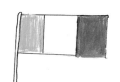

Shaun O'Connell
Scoil Phádraig Naofa, Dunmanway.

'James Crawford Neill worked as a library assistant in the National Library of Ireland in Kildare Street. He was a poet, a pacifist and a Presbyterian, and was about to be married in 1916. On Tuesday Easter week he was … avoiding Sackville Street by walking up Liffey Street, the family story goes that he came across children looting a sports shop and warned them that they might be shot for what they were doing. However, one of the children had an air rifle from the shop in his hand and it discharged a pellet hitting James in the spine. He was taken to nearby Jervis Street Hospital in general good humour and spirits with a relatively minor injury. His condition gradually deteriorated, however, and he died on the 10th of May. Shortly before he died he asked the hospital chaplain to perform the wedding ceremony to his fiancée … but the priest refused as the bride will soon be a widow.'

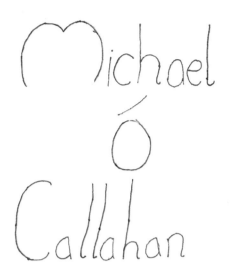

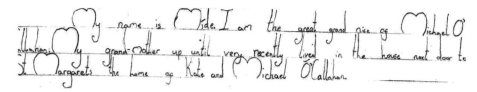

'Michael O'Callaghan was a city councillor and was extremely interested in Limerick's industrial life. He became Mayor in 1920.

He received two threats to his life, the first one just after the funeral of the Lord Mayor of Cork. His home on the North Strand, St Margaret's, was raided by two drunk policemen who told Kate that Michael would soon know more about murder after the incident. Michael would occasionally stay at the Royal George Hotel, however, on the 7th of March about midnight, Kate and Michael had gone to bed when they were suddenly awoken by two men banging on the front door. They shot Michael and in the confusion they shot Kate in the arm. The men fled the scene and within 20 minutes they shot George Clancy, Michael's successor as Mayor. Some years later it transcribed that the two men that had been murdered were both shot by the Black and Tans.'

Míde O h-Icí
Kilcolman National School.

Town clerk arrested

'In 1916 he was 27 years old and his job was town clerk of Drogheda. He was in charge of a group of rebels in the town and the British soldiers were stationed in Millmount overlooking the town.

He didn't fight with the men in Dublin at the GPO that Easter day but he did travel to Dublin the next day to take part. Joseph managed to escape the soldiers, mainly because of his job which was an important one in the running of the town and he worked for the authorities which gave him a certain amount of protection. However, by 1916 his luck had run out and he was arrested in Drogheda along with a number of men from the town and was transported to Wandsworth prison in England.

Because he was a town clerk and good at his job, the authorities in Drogheda requested his return to keep the town of Drogheda running smoothly. He was released nine days later.'

Amy Wilde
Scoil Mhuire National School, Schull.

Karol McCarthy
Lisavaird National School.

Leo Murphy was a member of the IRA.

On the 27th of June 1921, the locals were in the local pub on Waterfall after a days bowling. Word had got out, that the British Army (Essex Regiment) were on there way to shoot Leo. Beforehand, everyone in the pub put there guns behind the bar or else they would have been shot. Soon after, the British Army came. Leo tried to get out the back door but it was locked so he ran out the front door, jumped over a ditch but got shot by the British Army. Everyone in the pub, including my great granfather, Michael Forde were made walk over Leo's body and put in jail for 11 months. Some were only 16 years old.

Great anger and regret

Grace O'Neill
Gurraneasig National School.

'On the weekend of the 1916 Rising, they were all preparing to take part in the Rising in the Cork area. On the morning of Easter Saturday, they all met with a number of other local IRA members at my great grandfather's house in Clonbouigh … However, there was an order from a leading IRA member Eoin McNeill telling them that the Rising was cancelled … After a long discussion, the Battalion leaders reluctantly gave orders for the members to return home, much to the disgust of my great grandfather and great gran uncles …it was with great anger and regret when they found out that the Easter Rising went ahead'

The French officer's jacket

The volunteers also raided wealthy houses like Kilcaskin Castle and Conors of Manch for gun powder, guns, blankets, clothes etc. When the volunteers raided Kilcaskin Castle Paddy found a French Officer's jacket. Paddy's Aunt fitted the jacket to him. Tom Barry saw the jacket on Paddy and asked him if he could use it.

Maebh O'Brien
Ballinacarriga National School.

This photo was taken of Paddy when he was 24 years. He is wearing a French officer's jacket. The jacket was later worn by Tom Barry in The Kilmichael Ambush.

Spud Murphy

Jim Murphy and Jim Lane from the I.R.A were on the run and came into Rosscarbery. They were hungry so they went into O'Regans Pub. Cathy O'Regan knew them and gave them each a meal and a drink. When the men were eating Cathy saw The British Army drive into the square of Rosscarbery. She warned the men and they ran out into her garden and hid under potato stalks for two days. Cathy's brother, Pat gave them each a bar of chocolate and offered them a meal and a drink. They declined this offer because they might be found. They told Pat not to return to the garden as The British Army might suspect that people were hiding in the garden. The British Army questioned Cathy did she see any men around but she gave no information. The British Army still checked the garden but never realised that Jim Murphy and Jim Lane were under the potato stalks. The British Army remained in Rosscarbery for quite a while. Jim Murphy and Jim Lane decided to escape during the night. They eventually walked to Rosscarbery Pier. They found a local man with a boat to take them across to Galley Head, from there they made it a safe house at Fisher's Cross. Back in Rosscarbery twenty-six British Army men demanded food and drink at O'Regan's Pub. Jim Murphy was nicknamed Spud Murphy after this happened.

Claire Griffin
St Joseph's GNS, Skibbereen.

Cathy O'Regan was my great-grandmother.

Learned to knit

During these troubles, my great grandad was on the run in West Cork. He was shot in the thigh in Clonakilty and he made his way across fields to a farm where he was taken care of in an outhouse and was later moved on to a safe house. The wound left him with a limp for the rest of his life. He had a lucky escape also in Crossbarry when a grenade rebounded off a tree and landed at this feet. He spotted that the pin was still in, so he pulled the pin out and threw it back from where it came!

He didn't talk a lot about the Civil War as it was so divisive, but in his later years he pointed out many safe houses in West Cork. He learned to knit while on the run which was unusual for a man but must have kept him warm and busy.

Johnny Walsh
Rathmore National School.

Clean off the blood

While in prison the Black and tans shot
Canon Thomas Magner and 23 years
old local man Tadgh Crowley, 1 mile
east of Dunmanway. Their bodies
were brought to Dunmanway poor
house on stretchers. Their bodies
were put on tables

Mick Fitzpatrick
was given the job to clean off the
blood with water and rags. He failed
to get the bloodstain off the table.
This memory stayed with him all his
life.

Eloise Fitzpatrick
Reenascreena National School.

'While in prison, the Black and Tans shot Canon Thomas Magner and 23 years old
local man Tadgh Crowley, 1 mile east of Dunmanway. Their bodies were brought to
Dunmanway poor house on stretchers. Their bodies were put on tables.

Mick Fitzgerald was given the job to clean off the blood with water and rags. He
failed to get the bloodstain off the table. This memory stayed with him all his life'

He told no one

My great-great grandfather was part of the
old I.R.A and fought in the War of Independence. My
great grandfather would hear him leaving in the middle
of the night, only coming back many hours later. He told
no-one of where he went or what he did. He once
cleared some trees for an attack on the Black and
Tans, but we do not know if he actually took part
in the attack.

Kayla Collins
Drimoleague National School.

Saved by a rabbit

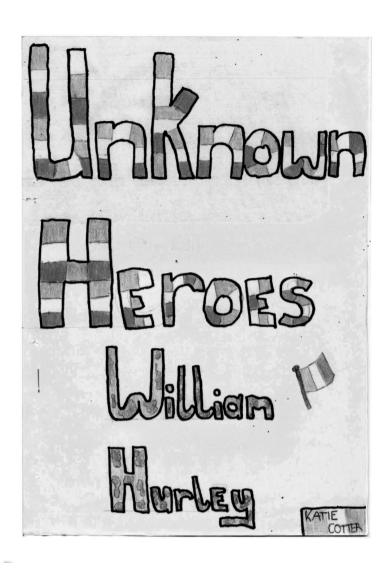

One memory Bill passed onto his children was about the time he and his comrades were ordered to cut up a bridge or a section of road near Castletownkenneigh. They were hard at work when they heard vans coming from the distance and they knew it was to be the Black and Tans. They all ran for their lives. Bill said that he dived into the bushes for cover and as he did a bullet hit a rabbit killing it. Bill realised that that rabbit saved his life. He did this job on a regular basis, but this was the only story he told his children.

Katie Cotter
St Mary's Senior School, Dunmanway.

Buckle saved his life

Eva Pattwell
St Joseph's Girls National School, Clonakilty.

Anne can remember when her brother Jack got shot on his thigh in a bog between Lyre and Ballineen. Jim Hurley from Clonakilty another active member of the I.R.A at that time carried Jack on his back out of the bog. Jack was taken to a safe house in Crossbarry. In the house he was dressed as a pregnant woman wearing a long black cloak and a head scarf to disguise him. Jacks first cousin John Corkery who was on the board of the North Infirmary Hospital organised for him to be taken in the back door (which was the kitchen door). The bullet was then removed from his leg.

Kerry Coombes
Knockskeagh National School

Dylan Lynch
Dromleigh National School.

Dressed in nun's habit

There was once a solicitor named Mr Jasper Wolfe. His father was the local shopkeeper and also Methodist. Jasper Wolfe was made Crown Solicitor. Basically he brought criminals of small crimes to court for the British Government. He lived in Norton House on North Street in Skibbereen. (now in 2017 this is used as a planning office by Cork County Council).

The IRA sent people to kill Jasper for bringing Irish people to court. But, as many times as they tried, they failed!

Mrs MacDonald was Japer's neighbour and she worked as a domestic in the local convent. On one occasion when Jasper was home and the IRA came to kill him, Mrs MacDonald came to his rescue. She entered his house through a back door, bringing with her one of the nun's habits off the washing line. She dressed him in the nun's habit. They got out of Skibbereen to safety. Mrs MacDonald's daughter went to work for his legal practice years later.

Fionn Coombes
Abbeystrewry National School, Skibbereen.

The Sacred Heart picture in my Nana's house

This story is about the man who put the Sacred Heart picture in my Nana's house. When she first got married she wanted to change the picture because it was to big but she was told "No" because it was hung there by Pat McCarthy.

Pat was a soldier who fought with the IRA during the war of Independance and was part of, Tom Barry's Flying Column in the Battle of Kilmichael. Later, during the Civil War he was trying to take Skibbereen from the Free state by shooting at the R.I.C Barracks.

After a long time shooting, Pat decided to take a break. He lit a cigarette, sat down and relaxed. Little did he realise that the smoke gave away his position and he was shot dead. He was later buried in Aughadown graveyard where he still lies to this day. So now, when I see the Sacred Heart picture in my Nana's house and remember the brave soldier who put it there.

Conor Casey
Lisheen National School.

Skin came away with the sock

In 1921, when Patrick Bohane, my Godfather's uncle was about 23 years old, he fought in the same unit as a man called Tom Barry.

Patrick's rifle was found in Bantry after a fight with the Black and Tans, and the story came back to Sean's grandmother that Patrick had been killed. His family were going to Bantry when they met another famous soldier in the Revolution, Neilus Connolly, and he told them that Patrick wasn't dead. So they turned around and went home. And, an evening or two later, all the neighbours were gathered in the house. There was a bit of a party because Patrick was still alive. And then, Patrick arrived at the house. He went to the big open fireplace in the old farmhouse and took off his shoes and socks and the skin from the souls of his feet came away with the socks. That was because he had been travelling day and night through bogs and back roads. He had travelled from Bantry on foot because if he was found the Black and Tans would have killed him. So that was the story of Patrick Bohane. The war ended and he survived. He moved to Boston in America and came home once in 1954. And that was the only time my Godfather met him.

Daniel Greenham Taylor
Gaelscoil Dhochtúir Uí Shúilleabháin, An Sciobairín.

- Rugadh Seán Sabhaois i gCathair Chorcaí i 1906.

- Bhí sé ina chonaí i 4, Ballymacthomas, Corcaigh. (in aice Sráid an mBlárna)

- Bhí sé i bhall de Fianna, Éireann chomh maith. Bhí sé sa "D Company, First Battlion, First Cork Brigade."

- Ní raibh sé ach trí bliana déag d'aois agus bhí sé ag faire nuair a raibh na fír feasta ag cleachtadh in aice Páirc an Aonaigh agus Droichead Croic Baile Átha Cliath.

Cé go raibh sé óg, bhí air beith freagrach agus iontaofa. Dúirt sé le rúnrail go d'oibrigh sé mar reathaí agus teachtaire. Bhí sé sin dáinséarach i gCorcaigh idir 1919 - 1920. Cé nach raibh na daoine feasta é a deanamh bhí orthu buachaillí óga, cosúil le Seán a úsáid. Táim 11 anois agus ní bheidh mise ag déanamh rudaí mar sin!

Stíofán Tóibín |
Gaelscoil Dhroichead na Banndan. |

My Grandad's family, The McCarthys were known as the Straics. 'Straic' is short for 'Straicaire' which is Irish for big and strong and they were all that way. They lived in a Glen with a lake near Ardgroom called Glenbeg and they didn't believe in fighting. They were pacifists.

During the War of Independence the IRA came to the Glen to force them to fight on their side but they wouldn't. The IRA started shooting at them and the McCarthys were surrounded in their hayshed. So they started shooting back. After a long battle they scared the IRA off and they gave up and went away. They never came back, and the McCarthys never fought again.

Aidan Davison |
Scoil Eoin National School, Innishannon. |

Timothy played an active part of delivering secret dispatches to the flying column. It was dangerous to post letters as all suspicious letters would be opened and there were no phones back in those days. As he was a farmworker he could move freely around the countryside. He hid the messages in his shoe for if they were found he would have been shot on the spot.

Grace Gallagher |
St Joseph's GNS, Skibbereen. |

Edith Somerville's sword

At around 1922 my great great great Aunt Edith Somerville had a sword on her wall, in the hall.

As Edith kept the sword, two men from the I.R.A came. They requested it and wanted it for battle. Willingly and gladly Edith gave them the sword and they scampered down the drive.

That night Edith had a dream, about the sword being thrown into a bush. In that very morning, she went to the bush that she dreamed about, and looked all over it.

She came back .... to Drishane (home) with the sword in her arms. And we have kept the sword on our wall, in the hall, in Drishane house ever since.

Hal Somerville
Abbeystrewry National School, Skibbereen.

His family never asked

'Timothy McCarthy was born in 1892. He had six brothers and six sisters. Between 1916-1923 most of his brothers and sisters emigrated to America during those years as there was no future for them here. Timothy was the only one to stay in Ireland to run the family farm and look after his parents. When the 1916 Rising started he joined the local army. He received medals from the Irish government. Later in years he never spoke about what he had done and his family never asked him.'

Shauna McCarthy
Caheragh National School.

Once they returned home to Innishannon they decided to stick to farming and give up their heroic past too!

Samuel Linehan
Scoil Eoin National School, Innishannon.

Refused pension

Cornelius O Mahony refused to collect a pension for his services as he didn't believe that he should be paid for what he did for his country.

Róisín Curtin
Scoil Eoin National School, Innishannon.

Aftermath

. My Nana and Grandad now live in the house the IRA stayed in.

. The IRA man left Ireland straight away and went to America.

. Once in America the IRA man worked on railways.

Saoirse Horgan
St Joseph's National School, Dromore.

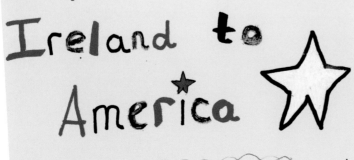

Ireland to America

earóid Ó Súilleabháin

Denis Cadogan
St Joseph's National School, Dromore.

Our interest in Gearóid Ó Súilleabháin began when we discovered he was born in Coolnagurrane Skibbereen, our town land. He was actually born next door to one of us. At first it didn't really mean anything to us but as we learnt more about his life and achievements we began to feel it was a great honour. We would imagine that Coolnagurrane has changed an awful lot since Gearóid's time - the road would have been a boreen more suited to horse and carts than cars. There was a big wood on the boreen which was cut down in the 1950s by Fullers Sawmills, Skibbereen. As his home in Coolnagurrane was raided many times by the police, you would wonder did he use the wood to hide in. One of our neighbours remembers when he was young helping his father to clear the rubble of the house and the rubble was used as part of the foundation of the house that our neighbours built on Gearóid's Site. He also remembers finding relics amongst the ruins, sadly these must have been destroyed as the didn't realise the importance of them. Over the years the site has passed from O'Sullivans

Michael Collins sulking in the picture with his family.

Anna Collins
Gurrane National School.

The first story is about why Michael was frowning in the only picture taken of him as a child.

It was around 1899 and Michael was living in Woodfield near my greatgrandfather Pattie Collins. They were cousins but also good friends.

One Sunday Michael was playing with Pattie and some other boys outside Patties house at Sam's Cross. It was a very exciting game of bowling, and Michael was winning, but before he could take the wining shot, his older sister Margaret came running down the road coming from Michaels house shouting his name.

"Michael! come quick! The Yanks are home and they're taking a family photograph."

"But I'm winning," he moaned.

"Now!" Margaret yelled and she took off up the road again. Michael told his friends to wait for him and reluctantly ran home after his sister.

When he got home he sulkily greeted his American cousins and stood in for a picture. Michael hardly took any notice of the new fangled, rare, fancy camera, and as soon as the picture was finished he rudely ran out the back door and pounded down the road to Patties house to win the game of bowling.

Forced to burn Collins' house

My Nanny was born in Sam's Cross in the same homestead as Joanna O'Brien who was Michael Collins's mother.

My Nanny heard about the burning of the Collins's homestead just down the road in 1921 when a detatchment of soldiers arrived and at Bayonet point forced a number of neighbours of which her father was one, to pile hay inside the house and outbuildings, douse them with petrol and set them on fire, Michael Collins's family were left homeless.

Callum Moloney
Scoil Naomh Bhríde, Union Hall.

On August 22nd 1922 Uncle Stephen met General Michael Collins.

Uncle Stephen described Michael Collins as the biggest man he ever saw. He wore a soldiers uniform with a long overcoat. He had jet black hair and piercing blue eyes. When he walked into the hotel people stepped out of his way in case he walked over them. The local army division all assembled in the courtyard of O'Donovans Hotel. Uncle Stephen watched them from an upstairs window. Michael Collins spent an hour shouting at the soldiers. Some people said they could hear him roaring at the other end of the town. When the soldiers left the yard they were pale, shaking and none of them could say a word.

Michael Collins stayed for a while in the hotel talking to locals and then left in the afternoon. At around 8 oclock that evening word came to the hotel that Michael Collins had been shot and killed at Beal na Blath. Uncle Stephen remembered how people were crying and all the workers in the hotel were told to go to their rooms and lock the doors for the night. It was very frightening for everyone. In the days that followed there were masses and prayers said for Michael Collins and that brought people together in their grief.

Aidan Connolly
Derryclough National School.

Marcus Adams
Derryclough National School.

Collins' last night

Jack Moore
St Joseph's National School, Dromore.

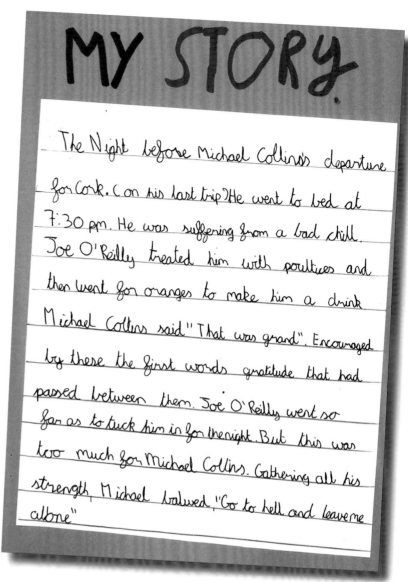

MY STORY.

The Night before Michael Collins's departure for Cork. (on his last trip)He went to bed at 7:30 pm. He was suffering from a bad chill. Joe O'Reilly treated him with poultices and then went for oranges to make him a drink Michael Collins said "That was grand". Encouraged by these the first words gratitude that had passed between them. Joe O'Reilly went so far as to tuck him in for the night. But this was too much for Michael Collins. Gathering all his strength, Michael bralwed "Go to hell and leave me alone"

Child's memory of the shooting

On Aug 22nd 1922 my Great Gran Uncle, Dan Holland, was the same age as me , 10 years old. He lived in Beal na mBlath in the only house overlooking the scene of an ambush that was to change the course of Irish history later that day. At noon on that summers day, his household received a visit from local Republicans advising to stay indoors and keep out of harm's way. A cart from a brewery was commandeered and an ambush was laid for a convoy that was coming in their direction from Bandon.

During the twilight hours he could hear the gunshots ringing out for 30-40 minutes whilst the ambush unfolded. He didn't realize the gravity of the events unfolding within earshot and he kept indoors to stay safe. The following morning, as he was going to the creamery he spotted a cap on the ground were Michael Collins was shot, later learning that it was Michael Collins' cap.

His story or that of his family was never documented properly and offers the potentially only independent witness account of the most momentous day in the history of the Irish Free State.

Keelin Holland
Scoil Eoin National School, Innishannon.

During the Civil War when Micheal Collins was shot, Jack was driving Eamonn De Valera in an area outside Fermoy, we think it was Araglen. De Valera was on a tour of the south boosting morale at that time. When they recieved news from an oncoming motorbike curier that the "Big Fellow" was shot, De Valera put his hands to his face and started to cry and said "poor Mick, poor Mick." When my great grandfather used to hear stories that De Valera was present when Micheal was shot in Béal na mBláth he used go berserk because Eamonn was with Jack.

Kevin Dart O'Flynn |
Scoil Eoin National School, Innishannon.

My great grandad driving michael collins

Katie Daly |
Caheragh National School. |

Michael Collins, great friend of my great great grandfather John McCarthy and a hero to all his family. Jack died on the 22nd August, 2003. A great Michael Collins man all his life it was a coincidence that he died on his anniversary. He would have liked that!

Liadhain Ní hÓgáin |
Scoil Naomh Bhríde, Union Hall. |

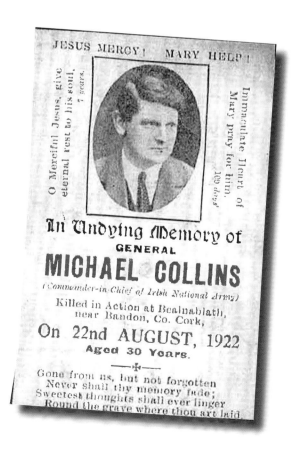

JESUS MERCY! MARY HELP!

O Merciful Jesus, give eternal rest to his soul.

Immaculate Heart of Mary pray for him.

In Undying Memory of
GENERAL
MICHAEL COLLINS
(Commander-in-Chief of Irish National Army)
Killed in Action at Bealnablath, near Bandon, Co. Cork,
On 22nd AUGUST, 1922
Aged 30 Years.

Gone from us, but not forgotten
Never shall thy memory fade;
Sweetest thoughts shall ever linger
Round the grave where thou art laid

Collins' car post ambush

Michael examining the Sliabh na mban at the curragh camp, 1980's.

Abbie Wedlock
St Joseph's Girls National School, Clonakilty.

Michael Murphy born November 19th 1898 in Cavan, Barrack Hill. Born to Cornelius Murphy from Rosscarbery (a Royal Irish Fusilier in the British Army!!!) and Mary Wren from Clonakilty.

After Michael Collins was shot at Béal na mbláth the Sliabh na mban (armored car) had to be abandoned from the retreating convoy. Michael Collins' body was transferred from the Sliabh na mban to the touring car to make the journey to Cork city.

The following day Michael Murphy and a small team were sent to find and drive the Sliabh na mban back to Bandon. When they found the car it had been stripped of its wheels, after much searching all four wheels were found hidden in fields. The car had to be put back together before making the journey

Michael Murphy
Transport District Officer
No.5

Who shot Michael Collins?

A friend of my Dads that lives in Douglas was in a house when he was very young with his father. The house belonged to his Dads friend. He was one of the men at the ambush firing at Collins and his men. This was in 1967. A fancy Rolls Royce pulled up outside the house. It was a film producer called Albert Broccoli, he was there to find out who shot Michael Collins. He signed a cheque that day and told them to write in whatever amount of money they wanted for the information. He tore up the blank cheque and said that he swore a pact the day of the ambush to take that information to his grave with him.

Alex O'Regan
Scoil na mBuachaillí, Clonakilty

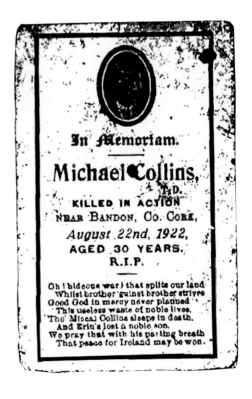

In Memoriam.

Michael Collins,
T.D.

KILLED IN ACTION
NEAR BANDON, Co. CORK,
August 22nd, 1922,
AGED 30 YEARS.
R.I.P.

Oh! hideous war! that splits our land
Whilst brother 'gainst brother strives
Good God in mercy never planned
This useless waste of noble lives.
Tho' Miceal Collins sleeps in death,
And Erin's lost a noble son.
We pray that with his parting breath
That peace for Ireland may be won.

John Paul McSweeney
Ballinadee National School.

THE IRISH CIVIL WAR

Séan Hales

Born: 1880
Died: 1922

Shane O'T
Kilcolman National Sc

Hales brothers.

About 1½ miles from my home, stands the Hales homestead and farm, here four Hales brothers were born and reared, Tom, Sean, Bill and Bob, all prominent members of the IRA. They also had a sister Madge a member of the Bandon branch of Cumann na mbhan.

Tom and Sean were officers in the flying column and all took part in the fighting. Their home at KnocKnacurra was constantly raided by the British army and eventually burned to the ground.

On July 27 1920 Tom Hales and Pat Harte were capured by the Essex Regiment at Laragh near Bandon. They were taken to a local farmhouse owned by a Hurley family, where they were questioned and when they wouldn't talk, were badly beaten. They were then taken to the Essex Regiment military barracks in Bandon, where they were brutally tortured. Tom Hales's finger nails were pulled off by using a pliars. The torture of Pat Harte was so severe that he lost his sanity and never recovered. He died in 1924.

Micheál Maguire
Ballinadee National School.

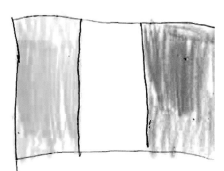

Sorcha Hurley
Scoil Eoin National School, Innishannon.

On the 20ᵗʰ August, the men were tried by court martial and sentenced to two years hard labour. Tom was initially, sent to Dartmoor Prison in England and later transferred to Pentonville Prison, where he eventually recovered from his injuries.

When the truce was signed, Tom came home to Ireland and then to his homeplace in KnocKnacurra.

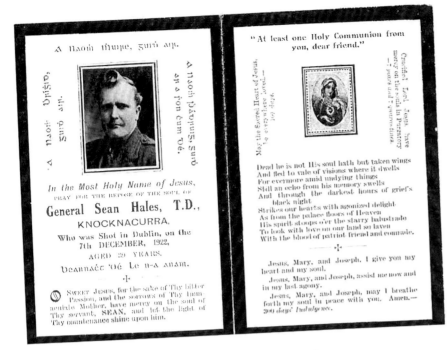

Liadhain Ní hÓgáin
Scoil Naomh Bhríde, Union Hall.

Sean Hales

Sean Hales was a great friend of my great great grandfather. He was also involved in the Irish Republican Army during the War of Independence. Sean Hales was elected to Dáil Éireann in both 1921 and 1922. Shortly after he was elected the Civil War broke out and on 7 December 1922 Sean Hales was killed by anti-treaty IRA men as he left the Dáil.

Two brothers fought on opposite sides

brother fought against brother. Here in our own Parish of Courceys the well known Hales family of Knocknacurra lived. They too were divided in their opinions against the signature of Michael Collins in London. The two brother Tom and Séan fought on opposite sides. Tom was against the Treaty while Séan was in favour of it. Séan was a T.D. and was assasinated in Dublin while alighting from his carriage. Following his death Mr. William T Cosgrave the Irish Primeminister ordered the death of four I.R.A. prisioners by firing squad. One was a teacher named Dick Barrett who taught at Gurranes National School near Crossbarry. My Granny Rita's Mother knew him and he would often help her to carry the bucket of water home from the well. She also had a copy of his last letter written the night before his exeution and which my Granny Rita now has. Michael Collins who negotiated the treaty with Lloyd George who was killed in an ambush at Béalnablath at the age of 32. It was a very sad time for all in Ireland. Sean Hales is buried in the old graveyard in the village of Innishannon and his grave is beautifully kept.

Leah Collins
Ballinadee National School.

This is the letter written by Madge Hales, my great grandaunt to her brother Dónal Hales, who lived in Genoa, Italy

This letter describes graphically the terrible burning of the Hales homestead by the Black and Tan soilders in March 1921

Madge Hales, from Ballinadee Bandon. Co. Cork, came from a Republican family and and all of her brothers- Seàn, Tom, Robert, Liam and Dónal (Dan) — were involved in the Irish Republican movement. Tom Hales was O/C of the 3rd West Cork Brigade until his arrest in July 1920. Seàn Hales O/C of the Bandon Battalion. Madge was a courier for Michael Collions and took regular trips to Italy to her brother Dónal who was a republican envoy in Genoa, Italy. Madge went to Italy to secure arms for the Irish cause and also to give her brother Dónal information which he could use for propaganda purposes on behalf of the Irish Republican movement.

Knocknacurra
8/3/1921

My Dear Dan,

Instead of the happy girl I was when I wrote to you last, I am now a homeless and almost a fatherless girl. The best and most loving of fathers is I must tell you with a breaking heart, waiting for his call to his happy home, where the English government cannot interfere with him. Oh dear father what you have seen in your last days, the home you made have been burned to the ground. And oh how heart pearcing to think that he was turned out of his dying bed without nothing to keep his poor body from cold and rain, with nothing even on his feet (but his bed socks). I will never froget his petitions to those heartless masked men. He said he was a dying man and asked for time to crawl downstairs with my mother, maid girl's and my help. The answer he got was we do not care what you are, only clear out quickly. Five minutes we got to clear with our lives. I had to drag poor father down to the workmen's house under cold and rain with terror in my heart, fearing when they got us inside they would again follow us. We were not out, when the house which they had sprinkled with petrol was bombed immediately, went on fire. The first bomb went off in the parlour as we just pass east. Thanks to the kindness of poor Pake Flynn, father was immediately put into bed and wrapped in warm blankets. Only for this he would have lost his life that night.

Séan Hales was my great grand uncle and he was the brother of my great grandfather Tom Hales. My grandfather Tommy Hales was born and lived in the home of Séan Hales, Knomacurra, Bandon, Co. Cork.

During the Irish Civil War (1919-1921) my great grand father Tom and my great grand uncle Séan fought on oppisite sides. Tom Hales Commanded the flying Column which attacked the free state army at Béal na Bláth which resulted in the death of Micheal Collins.

In 1921 Séan Hales was elected a TD in the government and he was shot dead in Dublin on his way to the Dáil because he was investigating the death of Micheal Collins.

In revenge for Séan Hales Killing, four republican Leaders were executed on 8th December, one from each province - Dick Barret for Munster, Liam Mellows for Connaught, Joseph McKelevey for Ulster and Rory O'Conner for Leinster. The Hales family did not agree with this.

The Hales family did not agree with this and they sent this letter to the "The Cork Examiner" newspaper which was published.

Sir,

That we view with horror and disgust the execution of the four Irishmen, Richard Barrett, Liam Mellows, Joseph McKelvey and Rory O'Connor, as a reprisal for the death of Séan Hales, our dearly beloved brother, and we think it a criminal folly to believe that such methods will end the strife in our land; and we are of opinion that reprisals on either wide will only increase the bitterness and delay the reconciliation that all patriotic Irishmen long and pray for, and also that the sole testimony of a British officer is very insufficient proof of how he met his death.

Shane O'Hare
Kilcolman National School.

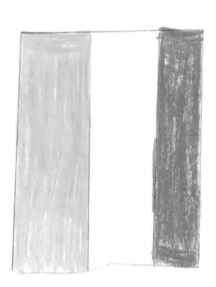

Jack Hennigan
Ballinacarriga National School.

Paul Madden
Scoil Mhaoilíosa, Knockavilla.

Caheragh Farm in 1921

Tom Barry was a wanted man. The war of Independance raged on in Ireland during the summer of 1921. Barry's ability as guerilla leader was well known in the IRA and also by the British forces.

The President, Eamonn de Velera summoned Tom Barry to General Headquarters in Dublin on 19th of May with a detailed account of the military position in the south. This journey was going to be extremely dangerous for him as he could be caught and killed at any time. It was decided that he would travel by train to Dublin while pretending to be a medical student. He would be given some medical supplies to help convience the enemy of this. Also he was to receive his only civilian suit from Cumann na mBan in Ballydehob. This was to be delivered to column headquarters in Caheragh. The headquaters were at the farm house of John McCarthy and his aunt Mary McCarthy of Letter, Caheragh. John had died in Cork on 13th of November but thanks to the help received from Joe McCarthy and Dan O'Donoghue of Drimoleague they called to the home of his brother Con instead on the 16th of May. Con McCarthy was a member of the Skibbereen battalion.

Tom Barry and his men slept outside on rubber sheets on the ground about 250 yards from the house, It was hidden by briars. They thought it was too dangerous to sleep in the house. in case it was being watched by the British. After a few hours sleep they were woken with the news that many British soldiers were stopped

a few hundred yards down the road and were looking for Tom Barry. He quickly dressed and ran. He learned later that a scout carrying his suit was stopped 3 miles from Caheragh. His name was on the package in case it got lost along with his rank number. When the scout refused to give his destination, they stripped off some of his clothes. The officer then put the scouts clothes on. They called to lots of farm houses asking questions and eventually found the farm house where Tom Barry and his men stayed. Luckily for Tom Barry someone from a farm house that the officer came to realised he had been tricked and managed to warn Barry with help from others to the danger. In the end a tailor near Crookstown worked all through the night to make the suit and Barry got the train to Dublin.

When a training camp was set up at Kealkil, in the Bantry area, for the officers of the Skibbereen and Bantry battalions in October 1920 , the Skibbereen officers attended. The camp which was in charge of Tom Barry was carried on for about 7-10 days. At this time Christy was responsible for driving Tom Barry.

Katie Daly
Caheragh National School.

Aoibhinn Twomey
Drimoleague National School.

THIS IS THE ROAD THE IRA ESCAPED ON.

Saoirse Horgan
St Joseph's National School, Dromore.

Fighting in The GPO

John Mulhall
St Joseph's National School, Dromore.

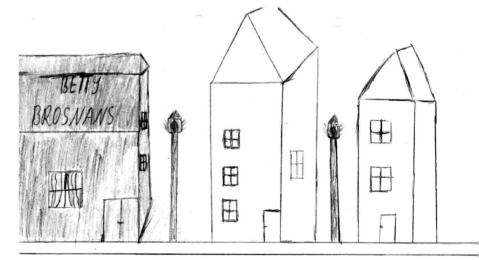

BETTY BROSNANS

Eoghan Minihan
Scoil na mBuachaillí, Clonakilty.

Chapter 4

CUMANN NA MBAN

The stories about this 'unique type of nationalist group' illustrate the vital role that women played in the revolutionary period, despite the potentially 'dangerous consequences' involved for both them and their families.

Lily O'Donnell Bradley
Gaelscoil Mhichíl Uí Choileáin, Clonakilty.

My great great grandmother was a high court magistrate in the republican court of Rathmines. She stood in for the men who were shot or in jail after 1916

Lily O'Donnell Bradley
Gaelscoil Mhichíl Uí Choileáin, Clonakilty.

Áine Heron was another woman active in the Republican courts. Máire Comerford, who described her as a 'brave, splendid woman', explained that as Áine had a large, growing family, the work suited her because she could do it while the children were at school. Áine Ceannt and Áine Heron sometimes sat together as justices for the Rathmines-Pembroke area, and on one occasion had their decision overruled. A money lender, who was also proprietor of a grocer shop, had brought a case against a number of women who had borrowed money to buy food from his shop and failed to repay him. The two justices calculated that he was getting 800 percent interest on his investment and they dismissed the case, announcing that they wanted the system of money lending discouraged. But Austin Stack, the Minister of Home Affairs, refused to accept this verdict, telling them that their duty was to uphold the law and not to condone departures from it. Áine Heron appears to have been a person of compassion and spirit, who refused to be overwhelmed by the rigmarole of court etiquette. On another occasion she angrily told a barrister who was aggressivly cross-examining a witness that she would no allow brow-beating, adding You must be fair this is not a british court.

Áine Heron's husband didn't know where she was the entire Easter week and he was very worried. Later she had a shop rented in his name: Heron & Lawlor, in Parnell Street, without his knowledge as a bomb factory and following an accidental explosion he was arrested after arriving home at Donnybrook from Upr. Baggot Street at lunchtime in 1920. They wanted to arrest Áine but she wouldn't release the baby in her arms.

Cunan na mban

uniform

This is a similiar fabric to the Cunan na mban uniform that my great great grandmother wore

Lily O'Donnell Bradley
Gaelscoil Mhichíl Uí Choileáin, Clonakilty.

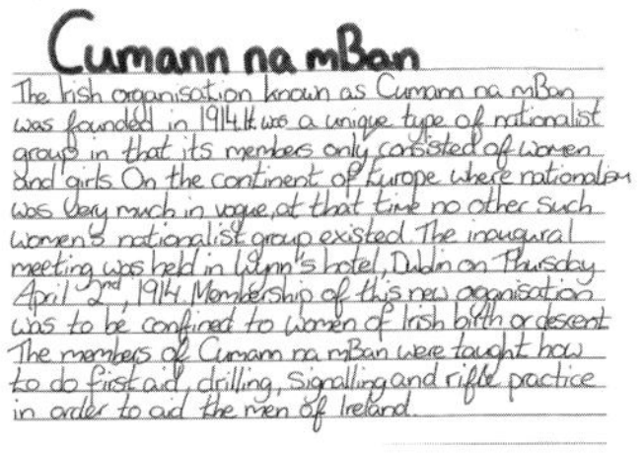

Cumann na mBan

The Irish organisation known as Cumann na mBan was founded in 1914 it was a unique type of nationalist group in that its members only consisted of women and girls. On the continent of Europe where nationalism was very much in vogue at that time no other such women's nationalist group existed. The inaugural meeting was held in Wynn's hotel, Dublin on Thursday April 2nd, 1914. Membership of this new organisation was to be confined to women of Irish birth or descent. The members of Cumann na mBan were taught how to do first aid, drilling, signalling and rifle practice in order to aid the men of Ireland.

'The Irish organisation known as Cumann na mBan was founded in 1914. It was a unique type of nationalist group in that its members only consisted of women and girls. On the continent of Europe where nationalism was very much in vogue at that time, no other such women's nationalist group existed … The members of Cumann na mBan were taught how to do first aid, drilling, signalling and rifle practice.'

Emma and Ellen Hurley
Rathmore National School.

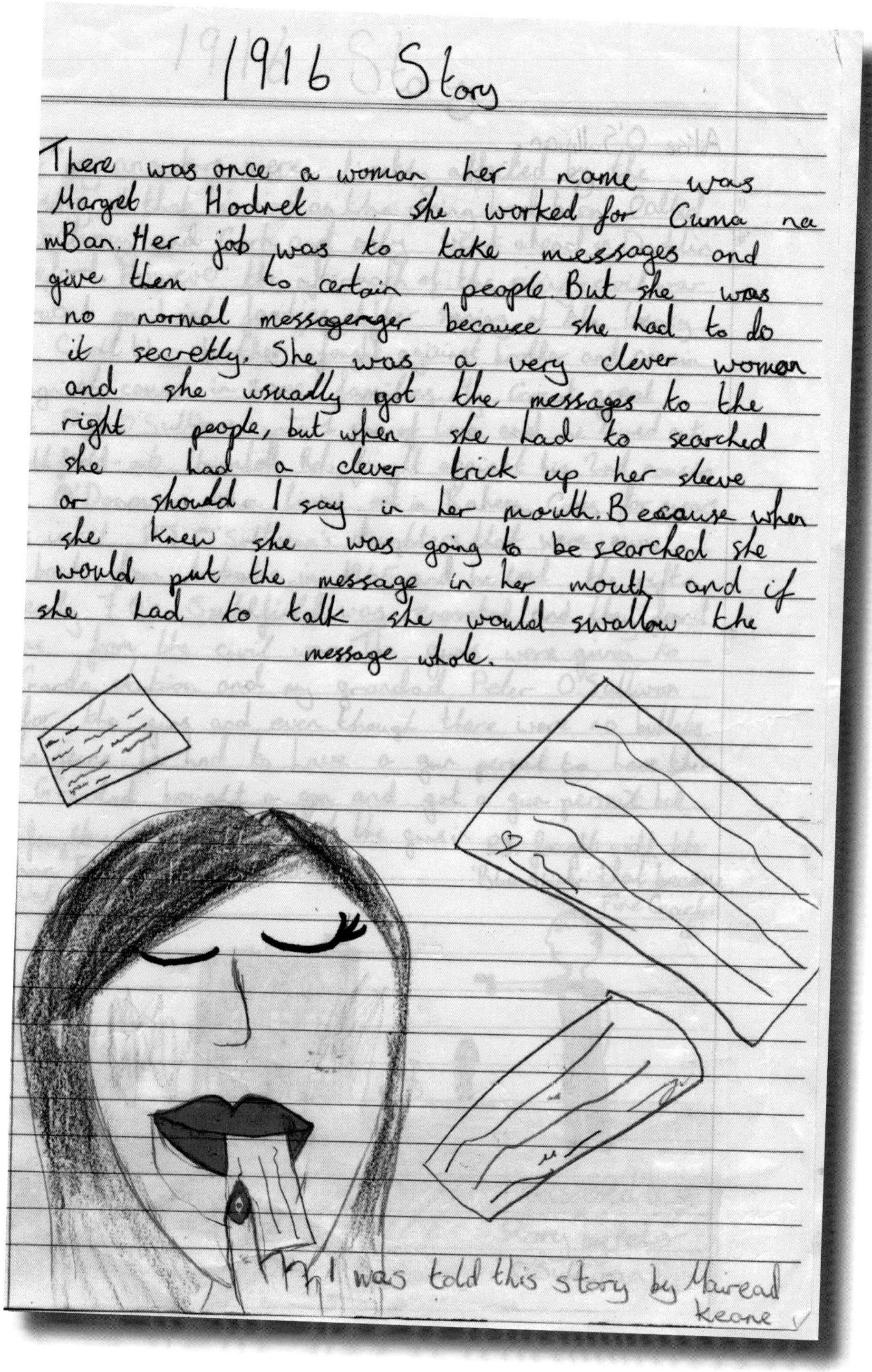

1916 Story

There was once a woman her name was Margret Hodnet she worked for Cuma na mBan. Her job was to take messages and give then to certain people. But she was no normal messagenger because she had to do it secretly. She was a very clever woman and she usually got the messages to the right people, but when she had to searched she had a clever trick up her sleeve or should I say in her mouth. Beacause when she knew she was going to be searched she would put the message in her mouth and if she had to talk she would swallow the message whole.

I was told this story by Mairead Keane

Ailíse O'Sullivan
Gaelscoil Dhochtúir Uí Shúilleabháin, An Sciobairín.

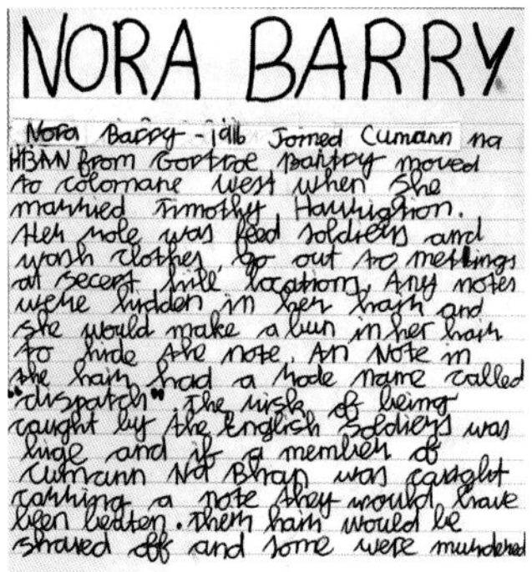

NORA BARRY

Nora Barry - 1916 Joined Cumann na mBan from Gortroe Bantry moved to Colomane West when she married Timothy Harrington. Her role was feed soldiers and wash clothes go out to meetings at secret hill locations. Any notes were hidden in her hair and she would make a bun in her hair to hide the note. An note in the hair had a code name called "dispatch". The risk of being caught by the English soldiers was huge and if a member of Cumann na mBan was caught carrying a note they would have been beaten. Their hair would be shaved off and some were murdered

'Nora Barry – 1916. Joined Cumann na mBan, from Gortroe Bantry, moved to Colomane West when she married Timothy Harrington.

Her role was to feed soldiers and wash clothes, go out to meetings at secret hill locations. Any notes were hidden in her hair and she would make a bun in her hair to hide the note. A note in her hair had a code name called "dispatch". The risk of being caught by the English soldiers was huge and if a member of Cumann na mBan was caught carrying a note they would have been beaten, their hair would be shaved off and some were murdered'

Sophie O'Sullivan
St Joseph's National School, Dromore.

Richard Bushe |
Rathmore National School. |

My aunt's granny (Mary McCarthy) joined Cumann Na mBan on the 7th of February 1921. They were difficult times in Skibbereen. One day Commandant Tom Barry asked for a woman in Skibbereen Cuman Na mBan to accompany him to carry out a reconnaissance of Skibbereen RIC barracks. This was not easy though as due to martial law no more than two people could be seen together and they had to keep their hands where everyone could see them. To top it all off there was a curfew from dusk to dawn! They enforced this law with something called bicycle squads. They were groups of R.I.C. soldiers that rode bikes at high speed to catch people outside after dusk. Mary McCarthy volunteered to help Tom Barry. Mary met Tom Barry. Tom explained the dangers but Mary still agreed to go. They arranged to meet the next day. Tom would be in disguise so he wouldn't be recognised. Mary was

told not to tell anyone. The next day Tom, Mary and Mary's father met at precisely 2pm. Tom explained the plan that Mary would lead the way on her bike followed by Tom who would be about forty or fifty yards behind. Then Mary's father would follow another fifty yards further back. Once they got to a tram way crossing Tom and Mary were to put their bikes into the tram yard. They would then proceed on foot toward Ilen St., around Goggin's Corner then down Bridge St on to Main Street through the square up High Street.

Mary and Tom proceeded towards the R.I.C. Barracks and turned right down by the mill and onto Market Street. Tom was not satisfied, so they went up Market Street and along the barracks again for another look at the lay of the land. Now there was over one hundred men of the King's of Liverpool regiment in the Town Hall, with up to twenty R.I.C. personnel in the barracks and always the chance of Tans or Auxies appearing in town which showed how brave Tom Barry really was. Having completed the circuit twice, they proceeded out Market Street. At the four crosses, they turned into Townsend St. From there they moved on to Dillon's Corner, turned left over to Ilen Street, then out to the tramway yard where their horrid journey had commenced. Mary's father could not have been happier to see her. The reconnaissance of Skibbereen R.I.C. Barracks and the military installation couldn't have gone better. It gave Tom a clear-cut knowledge of what he would have to contend later that night. I can't believe how brave Mary was!

Dangerous consequences

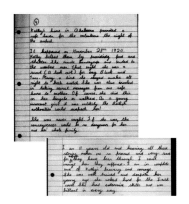

'Kathy's home in Ahakeera provided a safe haven for the volunteers the night of the [Kilmichael] ambush. It happened on November 28th 1920. Kathy helped them by providing food and shelter. She made bandages and tended to the wounded men. That night she was a scout (a look out) for any Black and Tans. Many a time she stayed awake all night to keep watch. She was also involved in taking messages from one safe house to another. Of course, she did this on her bicycle or walked. As a young innocent girl it was unlikely the British authorities would suspect her! She was never caught. If she was, the consequences would be so dangerous for her and her whole family.'

Anna Goyal
St Joseph's Girls National School, Clonakilty.

Sophie O'Sullivan
St Joseph's National School, Dromore.

Proud of my great grandmother

Cian Ring
Gaelscoil Dhroichead na Banndan.

Between 1916-1923 the Black and Tans would call to "Ardacrow House" many times. If the door was not opened to the Black and Tans, when they knocked at it, they would shoot at it. My Grandmother told me that she remembers growing up in the house as a little girl seeing the bullet marks on the door and being told the story of how they got there. Once the Black and Tans got into the house they would count how many chairs were in the kitchen or how many cups were on the table or in the sink and would ask how many people are in the house. If there were more chairs or cups on the table they would interrogate Helena and her sister. They would also try and see if there were any cigarettes butts lying around the house and in the farm yard and just like the chairs and tea cups in the house they would demand how many people are in the house or farm yard and if there are any farm helpers and demand who are they were and where are they. The Black and Tans would also demand who smokers were. Helena along with her sister also fed and cared for the injured IRA men who were hiding from the Black and Tans in their house.

Helena was awarded with two Cumann na mBan medals in the 40's by the Irish Government for her bravery, courage shown and demonstrated during the war of independence. I am very proud of Helena and very proud that she is my Great Grandmother.

My Great-Grandaunt, my Granny's Auntie, Hannah O' Neill was in the Eyeries Branch of Cumman na mBan which was formed in Spring of 1918 and also in the Eyeries Brigade of the IRA with her two brothers, Pat and Mick O' Neill, who answered to her even though they were older than Hannah.

Hannah, Pat and Mick and the rest of the Brigade decided to capture the Coastguard Station

On Sunday the 25th of July the brigade came and started to burn the place down. Some of the soldiers started shooting and there was a fight with shooting on both sides. Two soldiers were killed in the shootout. All of the other soldiers and their families left excepted for one lady who started to play her piano. She played 'Rule Brittania' while the whole place was burning down around her. When she finished she walked out slowly and collected her suitcase from Hannah and walked up the road towards Cobh towards the ferry back to England. Hannah thought the lady was great.

After that, Pat and Mick were deported to America but Hannah escaped and carried on burning. She was rumoured to have set the fire that burned down Puxley's Mansion at Dunboy Castle.

Aidan Davison
Scoil Eoin National School, Innishannon.

Emma and Ellen Hurley
Rathmore National School.

Scéal Fiona

Bhí mamó Fiona i gColáiste na Tionóide ag déanamh stadéir ar leigheas sa bhliain 1916. Iris Walton Long ab ainm di. Bhog sí go hOileán Chléire. Roimhe sin, bhí sí ina cónaí san Aifric. Bhí sí ag obair mar tiománaí trucáile le linn an dara cogadh domhanda. Ar eagla go cuireadh í faoi coisc tí, bhog sí go hÉireann arís. Sa bhliain 1965 bhog sí go hOileán Cléire.

Katy & Rowan Thomas
Scoil Náisiúnta Inis Chléire.

Hid them under the bed

My great, great grandmother Maggie Coffey O'Neill was from Knocks. She helped out the Volenters. She hid them under the stairs and bed. The Black and Tans were always around but the spies were even more plentyful but Maggie always managed to keep the Volenters safe.

Katie O'Mahony
Ballinacarriga National School.

Search suspicious Irish women

The rebels included brave women. Rebel women smuggled weapons inside their clothes, and British soldiers were to polite to search them. One officer suggested he could dress up his men as women and they could search suspicious Irish women.

Aoife d'Hondt
St Joseph's National School, Dromore.

1922

Dan Holland's

Great Escape!

These accounts document the harsh, and often inhuman treatment of prisoners at that time alongside the range of ingenious methods used to escape and avoid capture.

Calum O'Driscoll
Scoil Eoin National School, Innishannon

Held hostage on front of lorry

Jeremiah Fehily of Reavileen was arrested on the 26th January 1921 by Dunmanway Auxiliries near his home. He was beaten and taken to Ross R.I.C. Barracks. There he was accused of crimes by Sergent Twomey. When the Black and Tans and Auxiliries heard this, they hit him again and threatened him with revolvers. He was taken to Dunmanway and beaten and kicked on a regular basis. He was often taken out and placed on the

front of a lorry as a hostage and if they were attacked he was to be shot. He was taken to Cork, to Union Quay Barracks, to Victoria Barracks, Cork Gaol, to Spike Island and Bere Island. He was held until the truce.

Orlaith O'Flynn Meade
Kilcolman National School.

James & Catherine O'Callaghan
Leap National School.

Threatened on a train track

The old Muskerry Railway ran up beside the jail in those days and Michael and John L. were taken up the line and held there when the train was due. When the train was fairly close they were pulled off. This was done in the hope of getting information about the West Cork Brigade. They were later held in Spike Island and were beaten up many times.

Liadhain Ní hÓgáin
Scoil Naomh Bhríde, Union Hall.

Ava Scarlett
Leap National School.

The men were arrested and brought to a field where they had to dig out their own graves. The Black and Tans threatened the men and told them that if they caught them conspiring that they would be shot and thrown into the graves that they had dug. The men slept in the field that night. The Black and Tans came back the next morning and released the two O'Donovan brothers. Both of the Dalys

were made to march with the regiment to Owenachincha. The Dalys were then released but when they were walking home one of them got shot!

She also heard that around that time her father was arrested by the same soldiers and inprisoned in a prison in Dunmanway. He never talked about his day to day stay there but we believe it was not very pleasent. He was released after a number of weeks. It was said that he and a few other soldiers had to dig their graves — the idea was that if any of the other men were killed then her father and the other men would be killed in retaliation.

Callum Moloney
Scoil Naomh Bhríde, Union Hall.

Sáorlaith Murphy
Dromleigh National School.

Cons uncle, Bart Buckley of Castlehaven was arrested by Free State Soldiers from Skibbereen They went on a tour of some pubs. When they left Union Hall they were very drunk and when they reached Rineen Bridge they halted to check on

something they imagined on the right hand side of the road. In the confusion Cons uncle jumped over the bridge wall (20ft drop) down into the slob and in the darkness escaped to safety.

'Bart Buckley of Castlehaven was arrested by Free State soldiers from Skibbereen. They went on a tour of some pubs. When they left Union Hall they were very drunk and when they reached Rineen Bridge they halted to check on something they imagined on the right hand side of the road. In the confusion, Con's uncle jumped over the bridge wall (20ft drop!) down into the slob and in the darkness escaped to safety.'

James & Catherine O'Callaghan
Leap National School.

Muffled hooves

One night, Dan was crossing Baxter's Bridge in a horse and cart. He had covered the horse's hooves with pieces of material to muffle the sound of the trotting on the ground. Suddenly in the distance, he heard someone shout 'Stop!' He instantly knew it came from one of the Black and Tans and in that moment, he had to make a swift decision. He leapt out of the cart, over the stone bridge wall, and into the cold murky water.

He swam to the reeds in the river and hid among them for several hours until the Black and Tans gave up searching for him and left. Before they left, they fired several shots wildly into the reeds to see if they could hit or 'spook' him but they failed and he lived to tell the tale.

Calum O'Driscoll
Scoil Eoin National School, Innishannon.

A slippery escape

Jimmy Seán Crowley   20/11/17

Ciarán Brady asked Michael Brady

During the War of Independence, the British were rounding up all the men. When they got to Jimmy's house, they handcuffed him up, but before they took him away, he asked if he could wash himself first. They let him go back inside but while he was in there he covered himself in soap and then ran out the back door. The British tried to grab him but he was too slippy and got away. He moved to different safe-houses during the night and he got a blacksmith to take off the handcuffs.

He lived Ballinhassig

'During the War of Independence, the British were rounding up all the men. When they got to Jimmy's house, they handcuffed him up, but before they took him away, he asked if he could wash himself first. They let him go back inside but while he was in there he covered himself with soap and then ran out the back door. The British tried to grab him but he was too slippy and got away. He moved to different safe-houses during the night and he got a blacksmith to take off the handcuffs. He lived in Ballinhassig'

Ciarán Brady
Scoil Eoin National School, Innishannon.

At the time of the 1916–1922 troubles two of my great great grand uncles got involved fighting the British, not sure where, but they were caught and arrested. They were imprisoned in the Old Brothers School (St. Fachtna's De La Salle) upstairs. In the middle of the night they jumped out of the top window and got away, and went to America and didn't come back until they were old men.

Yasmin Atalay
Scoil Naomh Bhríde, Union Hall.

The O'Sullivan family were also directly involved with the Civil War. Two of the younger brothers, Denis and Pat, were captured by the opposite side and they were imprisoned in Skibbereen. They were to be sent for execution. The night before the execution the two brothers escaped the prison by jumping from a third floor window. They then went on the run for several weeks going from house to house owned by people on the same political side. During this time there were "safe houses" spread all over West Cork. These were also set up throughout the country. The brothers made their way from safe-house to safe-house unnoticed. After several weeks they finally made it to the town of Cobh. This was the main port in the South of Ireland where large shipping liners left destined for the USA primarily but also other countries and continents. Documents, travel papers and passports were organised for the two brothers by their allies to allow them leave Ireland and be allowed enter the USA. With Denis and Pat aboard, the liner left Cobh destined for Boston via Newfoundland, before reaching the American East coast. Their escape from certain execution was successful.

Mia & Nathan O'Sullivan
Ardfield National School.

So my great grandfather was fighting in the war and he was hauled into prison by the British soldiers during the war. He was in a cell with Kevin Barry. They were all going to be executed. However I'm sure that they didn't know that at the time. Anyway my great grandfather decided he would try to escape. He found a drain. So he decided he would escape through that. He asked Kevin Barry if he wanted to go with him. He refused and said he was too afraid he said he was too afraid to go with him. Kevin Barry was sent to his death a few weeks later. My great grandfather escaped, lived on, married and had my granny.

Niall Owens
Scoil Phádraig Naofa, Dunmanway.

Cheese, Cheese, Cheese!

Kadi Deasy
Gaelscoil Mhichíl Uí Choileáin, Clonakilty.

This prison was run by a brutal regime which was violently resisted by the prisoners. The main diet consisted of cheese and a bucket of water. Consequently, his family in later years, never saw cheddar cheese serve in Killarney as Batt couldn't stand either the sight or the smell of cheese after his time on Spike Island. Batt fashioned both a ring and a medal from silver coins while on Spike Island.

How is it. by Gods Decree
I'm cursed. outlawed and banned,
Because. I swore one day. to free.
My Trampled. Native Land.

Daniel O'Donoghue.

Ballinadee

Bandon

Cork.

South Camp

Frongoch. 10.11.16.

Ciara O'Donoghue
Ballinadee National School.

Michael McLean lived in Lowertown,Schull. Near Gaggin British forces captured Micheal in the house of Charlie Hurley and he reported him. They tortured him mercilessly (showing no mercy) Michael had not died in combat. Michael had injured his hand sometime after the Kilmicheal Ambush. He was sent off to go and find the residence of loyalists John and Annie Duke but didn't find them and on he way he was captured. This incident took place on the 8th of December, 1920. After they had tortured him for some years they murdered and shot him at the age of 23.

'Michael McLean lived in Lowertown Schull … British forces captured Michael in the house of Charlie Hurley and he reported him. They tortured him mercilessly (showing no mercy) … After they tortured him … they murdered him and shot him at the age of 23.'

Aoife Galvin
Kilcolman National School.

My great-grandfather spent the next couple of years in Bally Kindlar Internment camp.
Eventually being released after Michael Collins signed the treaty agreement with Britain. During his time in Ballykindlar he witnessed people being executed and being severly beaten. My great-grandfather and others had their fingernails removed as forms of torture.

Meadhbh Kiely
Scoil Eoin National School, Innishannon.

Chapter 6

SAFE HOUSES

Places of refuge were essential during the revolutionary period. These extracts show how such 'safe houses' operated, but also reveal the risks involved for both the hosts and the wider community.

Lucy Jane O'Driscoll
Drimoleague National School.

'My great grandad, also called Michael Collins, his family home was a safe house in Gortnasaggart, Bantry, Co. Cork.

My grandad told me that he remembers his dad telling of how on cold, wet nights he and his sisters were woken out of their sleep to give their beds to the Irish soldiers. My great grandad's mum would put on a fire and started baking brown bread. The boys in the house were sent out around the area with tilly lamps to listen for sounds for any English soldiers coming.

They had glass bottles in their hands with the bottom broken off them to blow into them to send the warning signal to get the Irish soldiers out of their bed to let them run out of the house and up the hill to safety. Luckily nobody was ever caught in the house and it really was a safe house for the men. Guns were dropped off for collection and notes to be collected by Cumann na mBan.

The soldiers took brown bread and glass bottles of tea with them when they left. The bottles of tea were covered with a hand-knitted sock to keep them warm. My great grandad and his family would say the rosary when they left for their safety.

It was always in darkness when the soldiers would arrive at the house. There was evenings when the soldiers enjoyed playing cards, singing songs, dancing and would have enjoyed drinking a bottle of stout before going to bed.'

Gavin O'Sullivan
St Joseph's National School, Dromore.

[handwritten notes]

James & Catherine O'Callaghan |
Leap National School.

'Safe houses where the IRA could sleep and rest were very important … One such safe house was the Buckley house in Gortbrac, Castlehaven which was Mr Con O'Callaghan's mother's home. In this house they had built a false wall about 2ft away from an existing wall in a downstairs room with a trapdoor into it from the bedroom overhead.

The IRA men could sleep in beds and if the British raided the house (which happened often), they just got out of bed and down the trapdoor to safety. The younger members of the family (which included Con's mother) were put into the beds vacated by the men on the run, so that when the British came in, there was no warm unoccupied bed.

When the Civil War started the Buckley family remained true to their Republican ideals and the house was raided by Free State troops. On their first visit, a Free State soldier went upstairs and stuck a bayonet down through the floor and went to check if it could be seen below. He knew about the false wall. The hospitality he received in that house was forgotten.'

[handwritten notes]

'[John L. O'Sullivan] stayed [in my great, great grandfather's safe house] for two days until it was safe to continue. He slept in an attic room that that was not accessible from inside the house, but the only entrance was on the outside from the roof which was hipped. The valley on the hip roof had a very small entrance that was not visible from ground level. John L. O'Sullivan went on later in life to become a fine gael politician and was elected to Dáil Éireann.'

Killian Collins |
Scoil Phádraig Naofa, Dunmanway.

The valley on the hipped roof.

My great great grandfather Thomas Crowley 1869-1946

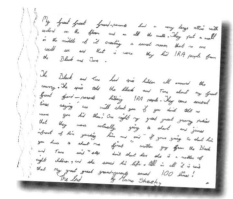

'My great great grand-parents had a very large attic with cardboard on the floor and all the walls. They put a wall in the middle of it creating a secret room that no one could see and that is where they hid IRA people from the Black and Tans.

The Black and Tans had spies hidden all around the country. The spies told the Black and Tans about my great great grand-parents hiding IRA people. They came several times saying "we will shoot you if you don't tell us where you hid them". One night my great great granny noticed that they were actually going to shoot and jumped in front of him guarding him and said "if you're going to shoot him you have to shoot me first". Another guy from the Black and Tans said "stop, don't shoot her she is a mother of eight children" and she saved his life. All in all it is said that my great great grand-parents saved 100 lives!'

Momo Sheehy
Gurraneasig National School.

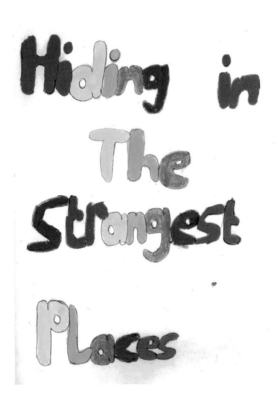

Ellie Buckley
St Mary's Senior School, Dunmanway

Jeremiah took up baking

Kate Connolly
Leap National School.

Hannah Connolly had given birth to her first child on the 14th January 1920. It was the practice at the time for women to remain in bed for three weeks after giving birth. When members of the 'Flying Column' came to the safe house, they always enjoyed Hannah's homemade brown bread. For the short time that Hannah was recuperating, Jeremiah took up baking the brown bread and everyone was very impressed!

The IRA would come and train on the farm, sleep in the barn and my great great grand aunts fed them cabbage, potatoes, brown bread, and sometimes meat. The women gave up their beds for the IRA to rest. One story is of my great great grandfather, who was sick in bed in 1921. His doctor, an English lady, was with him, when a dangerous British Lieutenent Perceival, rode into the farm yard, and ordered the place to be burned to the ground.

The Doctor stood up to Lieutenent Perceival and threatened that he better move on, before she Reported him. The house is still standing today with bullet holes in the barn wall as poof of the visitors at that time.

Naoise Quinn
St Patrick's BNS, Skibbereen.

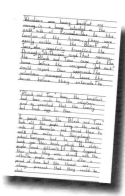

'Volunteers were having breakfast one morning, in a house situated on the north side of Reavouler. Due to the location of the house, they were easily visible to the Black and Tans who regularly travelled the Drinagh-Skibbereen road. That morning, the Black and Tans came to the home before the assigned look-out could report their approach. The volunteers managed to leave the house before they entered. The Black and Tans knew that the breakfast had been made for the volunteers and so insisted that the family boil fresh eggs for them.

To punish them, the Black and Tans took all the people living in the north side of Reavouler and forced them to walk two miles to Derryclough school. Everyone had to keep their hands over their heads which the older people found difficult. If they dropped their hands, they were struck with the rifle. The people were released after a period of time but the threat was always present that they could be shot.'

Kate Connolly
Leap National School.

Darragh O'Regan,
St Joseph's National School, Dromore.

Hideout with chickens

My great great grandfather Daniel o'connor used to live in Ballybrack Lodge in Douglas. During the war of independence he used to hide Irish Republican Army members who were wanted by the British in a secluded chicken coup that was across a stream at the back of their farm. The English never bothered to cross the stream for the fear of getting wet. So the chicken coup was a safe hiding place from the British.

Andrea Straub
Ballinadee National School.

They also used to hide people up the chimney breast in the front room.
There was room for one person to climb up inside the chimney and above the fireplace they would hang a picture of the Queen over the fireplace so that when the British forces called and saw the picture of the queen they beleived the household were loyal to the crown and would leave without searching.

Took his last breath

'The British commander seemed very confident that there was a Rep hiding in the residence and one by one he ordered the interrogation of each occupant individually in an outhouse. However, no information was forthcoming. With that, the BF commander ordered the soldiers to search all the outhouses but they had no success. All that remained to be searched was the barns. The soldiers fixed bayonets on their guns and began sticking the bayonets deep into the haystack in the barn. After a couple of minutes, frightened by the thought of being stabbed a young Rep, Paddy Crowley, made a dash out of the barn door in an attempt to escape capture. Before the soldiers realised it, the young man had made it half way across the adjoining meadow. The soldiers were soon in close pursuit. Being young and fit, and travelling light, young Paddy was soon getting further away as the soldiers' bullets rained in his direction but none getting close to the mark … Unfortunately for Paddy, a specialist marksman happened to be with the raiding party … eventually one of the marksman's bullets hit its target injuring Paddy's leg as he was running along the beet field. In an attempt to avoid further injury, Paddy fell to the ground and tried to crawl along the furrows using the beet leaves as cover. Over the next 15 minutes, the marksman continued to rain bullets where he thought Paddy was hiding.

Eventually a bullet found its mark and Paddy Crowley, 26 years of age, took his last breath and died. The occupants of the safehouse were subjected to brutal treatment by the BF for harbouring a known Rep fugitive. However, the pain of seeing young Paddy die far outweighed any pain that the BFs could inflict. The O'Neill house continued to be a safehouse as long as there were Reps on the run'.

Grace O'Neill
Gurraneasig National School.

Weak with the hunger

An old woman living by the Long Bridge in Dunmanway was known to give food and shelter to members of the Flying Column who would be weak with the hunge

Alex Coughlan
Drimoleague National School.

Chapter 7

ARMS DUMPS

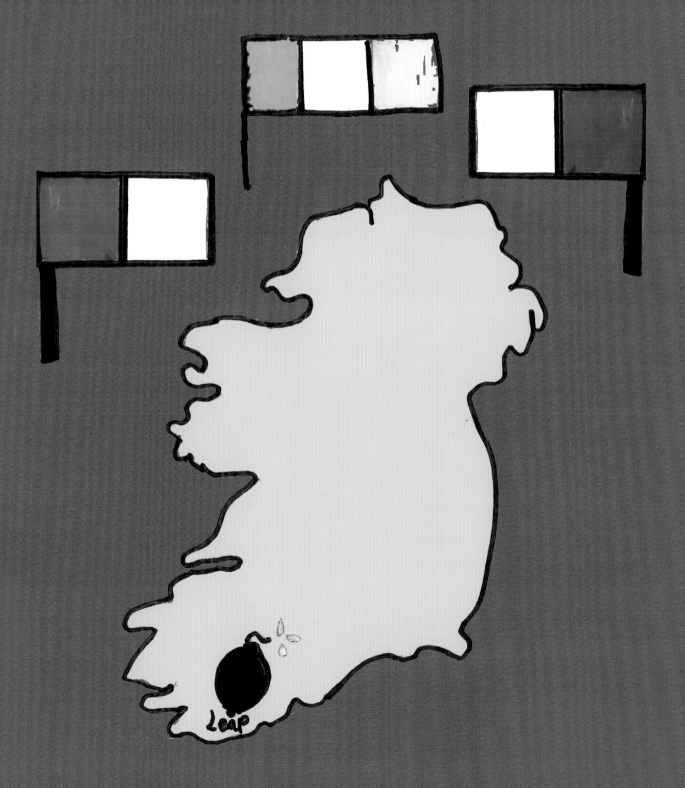

Access to munitions is vital in wartime, and this chapter reveals the many
varied locations used to cache arms at that time, including bogs, crypts,
underground bunkers, churns, blocks of wood and even coffins.

Katie Coughlan
Leap National School.

Bogs and biscuit tins

My Great Grandfather had an idea. He got a biscuit tin, much bigger than one's we have today and put the guns in the tin. Then he went to the bog, and cut out some sods of turf. After that he put down the biscuit tin in the hole and covered it with the sods of turf. When the Black and Tans came a few days later, his heart was in his mouth that the Black and Tans would find the guns but fortunately they didn't. My Granny said if they did find the guns they would have been sure to shot him.

Thank goodness for bogs and biscuit tins!

Muireann Nic Pháidín
Gaelscoil Dhroichead na Banndan.

Bullets in boiling pot

One day my great grandmother was in Riverlyons producing ammunition in the safehouse when the Black and Tans arrived She had no where to hide the bullets so she threw the bullets into a boiling pot of potatoes knowing that the bullets could blow up. She opened the doors to the Black and Tans knowing if they looked in the pot for food they would see the bullets and she would be killed instantly. Luckily they never looked in the pot and the bullets didn't blow up killing them all!

Aidan O'Dwyer
Lisheen National School.

Fake-bottomed coffins

'Richard's carpentry skill were used to make coffins for the undertaking business and also coffins with fake bottoms were used to transport shotguns and rifles safely because the British Army were slow to inspect coffins.'

Matthew O'Neill
Scoil Phádraig Naofa, Dunmanway.

Richard's carpentry skills were used to make coffins for the undertaking business and also coffins with fake bottom's were used to transport shotguns and rifle's safely because the British army were slow.

slow to inspect coffins.

The I.R.A. was a young organisation and members did not have the training, the equipment or the large numbers that the British army had. Guns and ammunition had to be hidden from the enemy in case they were taken from them. They were often hidden in reeks of hay, in the middle of heaps of turf, in out buildings or even in the inside of blocks of wood.

Pictured below is a block of wood that was used by my great Grandfather to hide his revolver.

A piece was cut off the side of the block of wood and a hollow was cut out of it. The side was screwed back on when the gun was inside to conceal the opening. An axe was placed near the block of wood and it looked just like a block for chopping wood on, rather than a hiding place.

Alannah Crowley
Caheragh National School.

Stored in crypt

Éanna Déiseach
Gaelscoil Mhichíl Uí Choileáin, Clonakilty.

He used to hide the guns in a underground crypt in the kilnagross graveyard. May Hayes recalls while on a visit to the Deasy Dairy the Black and Tans made a nerve-shattering raid but she had the good sense to hide a revolver in the base of their Singer Sewing Machine. They both supported the Anti-Treaty in the Civil War.

Guns and poteen

There was a bunker underground in the yard that was hidden well from the British. That kept all the guns for the IRA and the local men. That was never found. My grandmother often said we hid lots of stuff down there like poteen for the sick animals and of course the men and women who had the Flu.

John Paul McSweeney
Ballinadee National School.

Arms for Kilmichael

'There is a dome shaped stone on the farm where guns were hidden during the week of training [before the Kilmichael Ambush] in 1920. I recently made a visit to this with my grandad and took the following photos. The cave is approximately 2 metres in length and one metre in diameter at the widest point … It is positioned about 250 metres from the farm house behind a big rock in a secluded area.'

Orlaith Hickey
St Mary's Senior School, Dunmanway.

The Story of my Greatgrandad and my Greatgranduncle

Hidden on island

'During the Toureen Ambush there was no casualties. The Royal Irish Constabulary soldiers surrendered 19 guns and walked back to Cork. The 19 guns were later hidden in a small island in the middle of Annagh bog close to Crossbarry. The Royal Irish Constabulary could not get in to the island because there was a secret way in. The guns were then used in Crossbarry and Kilmichael ambush.'

Sorcha Kiely
Scoil Eoin National School, Innishannon.

Guns in churn

When my great grandad was 12 years old, he used to go to Michael Collins house and he used to clean the guns and load them up with ammunition for the next ambush.

When the soldiers were coming to raid Michael Collins house for the guns Timothy and his father would have already taken them away to their house.

They hid the guns in the bottom of the churn. When the soldiers came to the farmyard they couldn't find the guns as they were hidden in the churn. There was a false bottom in the churn.

Cathal O'Driscoll
Leap National School.

All companies of the volunteers had arm dumps in their area. One of these dumps was in Mr. Con Callaghan land. A pipe about a foot in diameter was placed in a fence and the end was covered with stones. This was six foot long and is capable of holding ten or twelve guns!

Zoe McInerney
Kilgarriffe National School.

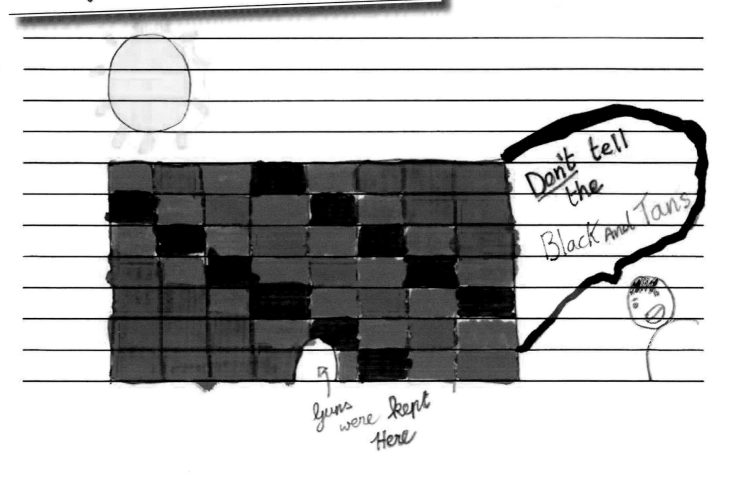

Don't tell the Black And Tans

guns were kept Here

One of my distant cousins, Trevor Ross Roycroft, who lived at 49 Townshend Street (where my Uncle Dick currently lives) was 14 during the 1916 rising. He wanted to join the Michael Collins free-state army but his parents refused to let him join and because he was under 18 he couldn't join without their consent. So his parents Thomas and Jennie, allowed ammunitions (guns) to be stored at the bottom of the garden about where the parking area is at the back of the current bicycle shop.

'There are several pictures of him during this period [including] in front of the Eldon Hotel with Michael Collins on the day he was killed … he is the boy in the front of the picture wearing a strange looking cap.'

Oran Roycroft
Abbeystrewry National School, Skibbereen.

That year the weather was poor and the turf was late being brought in, it was still in the bog. Back then the turf was stood in stacks, the Black n Tans arrived and went into the bog and kicked the turf around looking for the revolvers but they didn't find them as my Great Grandad had burried them on the bank of the bog by the drills. That night in the dead of the night James went out and dug up the relvolvers and burried them further on, on the farm in a place known as the dannagon.

My Grandad recalls being told the story when his Dad had the Relvolvers that were used in the Kilmichael ambush. They were wraped up inside sacks to keep them dry, and James Burried them in the bog.

Bog with stacks of turf.

Katie Scannell
St Joseph's GNS, Skibbereen.

The War of Independence

1921 The Black and Tans arrived into the farm yard of my great great grand father and great great grandmother Hurley from Teadies Upper Enniskeane. they were looking for guns and information on members of the family. they wrecked the house and broke furniture. But they never found the guns which were hiding in the ditch. they captured my great great grandfather and grandfather and took them to Dunmanway Jail. My great great grandmother and the young son were left to milk the cows, her husband and other son were held for two weeks and suffured severe beatings. When my grandmother was growing up her father told her this story and showed her markings on his legs from all the beatings they received in Jail, but they never told them where the older brother was hiding.

Caoimhe Craig
Gurrane National School.

AN SEAN GUNNA MEARGACH

Thart ar 1970, nuair a bhí m'athair ina bhuachaill óg, chaith sé an-chuid ama ag theach a uncail Dennis agus a aintín Cáit. Bhí feirm. Lá amháin bhí a uncail Dennis ag treabhadh, tháinig sé ar sean gunna meargach. Fuair an duine déarnach a bhí i bhfeighil an feirm seo an gunna le linn Cogadh na Saoirse. Bhí beirt fhear a bhí ag obair don I.R.A timpeall agus bhí an gunna acu. Bhí grúpa saighdúirí ar a thóir. Theastaigh uatha fáilt réidh leis an gunna, mar sin chaith siad an gunna sa pháirc taobh thiar den treabhadh. Bhí sé aimsithe arís timpeall 1970. Nuair a fuair uncail mo dhad é, bhí ana cuid mearg ar agus ní raibh aon adhmaid fágtha ar. 'Bolt action rifle' é agus tá seans ann gur 'Lee Enfield' a bhí i gceist. Bhí sé cómh h'ard le m'athair ag an am agus bhí sé an-trom freisin. Bhí an gunna i dtigh m'uncail ar feadh tamaill fada ach tá sé imithe anois.

Shane Langley
Scoil Náisiúnta Inis Chléire.

Cillian Keane
Drimoleague National School.

My great grandmother and great granduncles were O'Regans and they lived on a farm in Kealvine. On the farm, there was a hiding place otherwise known as a 'dump' where guns, ammunition and first-aid equipment was kept for the I.R.A..

A neighbour used to call to visit on Sunday evening and thinking he was their supporter my great granduncle took him and showed him their hiding place.

A week later eleven Black and Tans came along the back road from Dunmanway and stopped on the road at Upper Myrny Cross. They left their bikes and crossed over the fields at Touraheen and met a farmer by the name of Pasty Tom, ploughing a field with two horses.

The eleven Black and Tans soldiers asked the farmer did he know where the I.R.A. "Dump" was and he told them there was no such thing here. The Tans kicked him around the field and hit him with the stock of a gun. Then they took control of the horses and plough and ploughed in a criss-cross pattern over what he had done.

Pasty noticed there was a man with them wearing wire mesh goggles as a disguise and this man led them all the way down to the hide-out of the ammunition.

This man was the informer, the same man that used to visit my great granuncle's house on Sunday evenings.

16 years ago when my Mum and Dad were renovating the house I live in now the builders stumbled upon a cache of arms. These arms included a mills bomb, some shot guns, a revolver, hundreds of bullets and numerous detonators. These were all taken away by the Irish army bomb disposal unit. My great-gran uncle Cornelius McCarthy must have placed these in the dry, stone wall before the War of Independence truce. We know this because the arms dated back to 1921.

Ellie McCarthy
St Joseph's GNS, Skibbereen

My uncle lived in a house near Ballinascarthy in around 1975 Builders were repairing the house because it was old. They were taking off the roof when they found a sack, it was in the top right corner of the door frame. A Historian came out. He said 'there wouldn't be another one next to it? It would be opposite it'. So they checked. He was right. He put them both in a museum.

Emer Moroney
Kilcolman National School.

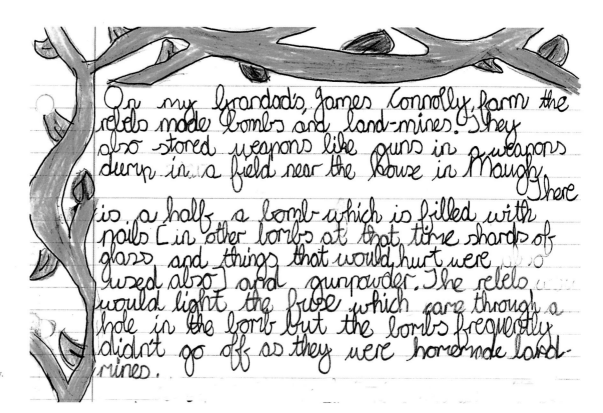

On my grandad's, James Connolly, farm the rebels made bombs and land-mines. They also stored weapons like guns in a weapons dump in a field near the house in Maugh. There is a half a bomb which is filled with nails [in other bombs at that time shards of glass and things that would hurt were used also] and gunpowder. The rebels would light the fuse which came through a hole in the bomb but the bombs frequently didn't go off as they were homemade land-mines.

Caoimhe & Maebh McCarthy
St Mary's Senior School, Dunmanway.

In the 1920's Aughadown Creamery was owned by the O'Regan family who went to Lisheen School. They used to make butter in the creamery and exported it to Wales. They used to bring back Coal which they used to sell in the creamery. They used to sail from Reenadina pier in Collatrum

They were supporters of the IRA and wanted to help the Cause any way they could so they decided to use the boat returning from Wales to import guns. The problem was that all boats would be checked coming into Ireland so they came up with a plan to take a very influential solicitor from Skibbereen who was a Unionist and supported the British. They offered him a trip to Wales where they wined and dined him and unknown to him they filled the boat with guns. On the return journey home they were stopped by British Customs Officers who saw the well known solicitor on board. They let the boat go without even checking it and thats how they got guns into Ireland to help in the fight Story told by my uncle William Casey

Molly Casey
Lisheen National School.

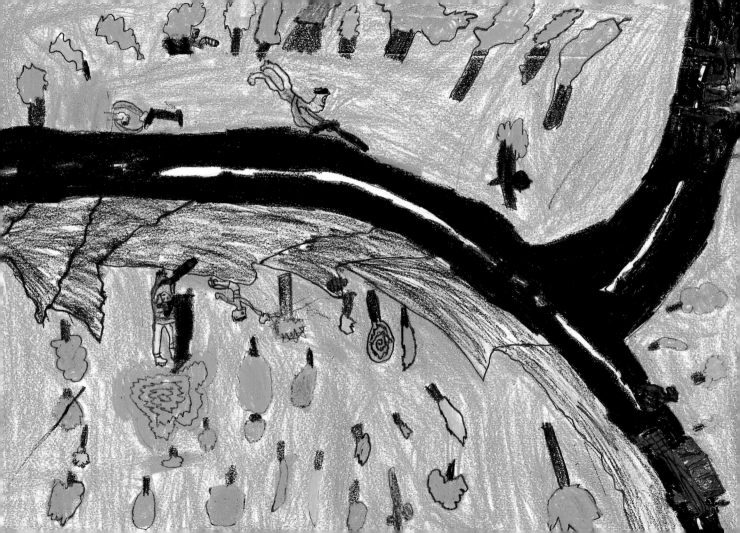

KILMICHAEL

Kilmichael Ambush

Abbie McCarthy & Laura Dullea
St Mary's Senior School, Dunmanway.

Pulled out of bed and shot

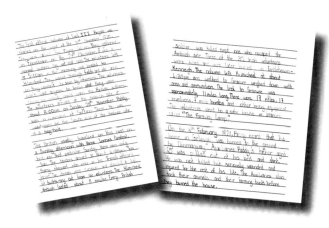

Maebh O'Brien
Ballinacarriga National School.

'The first official column of Cork III Brigade was started on the night of 21st [of] November 1920. They were called the Flying Column. They gathered in Enniskeane on the 27th of November. It was a normal winter's day, wet and cold. The volunteers left at 5am … and headed for Kilmichael. They walked through fields and old lanes so they wouldn't be seen by informers … The volunteers arrived at the ambush site at around 8am on Sunday the 28th [of] November. Paddy was in command of Section Three. He was positioned on the south-side of the ambush site in a bog-hole.

The British usually travelled on this road on a Sunday afternoon with three lorries (tenders), but on that particular Sunday there were only two. The tenders arrived at about 4pm. Tom Barry stepped into view in his French officer's jacket. The British were curious and slowed. A hail of bullets rang out from the volunteers. The Kilmichael Ambush lasted about 8 minutes. Every British soldier was killed except one who escaped the Ambush site. Three of the 32 Irish volunteers were killed and were later buried in Castletown-Kenneigh. The column left Kilmichael at about 4.30pm and walked to Granure weighed down with arms and ammunition. The trek to Granure was approximately 11 miles long. There were 17 rifles, 17 revolvers, 7 mills bombs and other heavy equipment. The volunteers went to a safe house in Granure called "The Faraway Camp".

On the 6th of February 1921, Paddy heard that his home … was burned to the ground by Dunmanway Auxiliaries. Paddy's father, aged 65, was pulled out of his bed and shot. He was not killed but seriously wounded and injured for the rest of his life. The Auxiliaries also took their animals and their farming tools before they burned the house.'

Conor Nash
Scoil Eoin National School, Innishannon.

On the morning of Sunday 28ª of November 1920, the Kelly family were getting ready to go to mass in Johnstown. It was a freezing cold winter day.

As they were leaving, a knock came on the door. It was Tom Barry telling them that he was taking over their house and that they could not attend mass that day. He ordered them to stay indoors and keep away from the windows and hide under the table.

They were terrified not knowing what was going to happen.

'My great-grandmother Nell Kelly was born in Gneeves, Kilmichael in December 1908. She was the eldest daughter of Timothy and Mary Kelly. She had four sisters … and five brothers … her father Timothy was a carpenter.

On the morning of Sunday 28th of November 1920, the Kelly family were getting ready to go to mass in Johnstown. It was a freezing cold winter's day.

As they were leaving, a knock came on the door. It was Tom Barry telling them that he was taking over their house and that they could not attend mass that day. He ordered them to stay indoors and keep away from the windows and hide under the table. They were terrified not knowing what was going to happen.'

- From 8am to 4pm, Nell and her family were held in their own home.

- Her brother Con managed to leave the house and go hunting rabbits with his neighbour Timmy Murray.

- During the day Tom Barry came looking for food for his men, who were frozen and hungry in their positions outside.

- The family sent out all the food they had which was brown bread and butter and a bucket of tea.

Eoin Hurley
Scoil Phádraig Naofa, Dunmanway.

A heavy stone was placed accross the road to slow down the crossley tender at the site of the present monument.

As evening fell scout no.3 John Kelly got a signal from scouts Daniel O'Driscoll and Tim O'Sullivan. to say the Auxiliaries were coming

The heavy sound of the crossley tenders warned the the family what was about to happen.

For fourteen minutes the sound of bombs and shooting rang through the air.

Nell and her family were terrified under the table. As the house was so close to the action bullets flew into the house knocking the white wash off the walls

After the shooting stopped Tom Barry returned to the house looking to remove the doors for streachers for the dead and dying. As Timothy Kelly was a carpenter he had doors in an outhouse and he gave them these door

After the fighting ceased the bodies of Michael McCarthy and Jim O'Sullivan along with the injured Pat Deasy were removed to Buttimers home in gathroe bog. Mrs. Buttimer looked after Pat Deasy until his death five hours later

Eoin Hurley
Scoil Phádraig Naofa, Dunmanway.

The Buttimers Home where Pat Deasy died

On Monday the 29th the Auxiliaries travelld from Macroom looking for their comrades. They removed sixteen corpses back to Macroom castle for post mortem.

One Auxiliaries survived and was confined to a wheelchair for the rest of his life.

- A temporary grave was dug for the three bodies in Gothroe bog.

Later that night the bodies were transferred by horse and cart to Castletown Kennagh. The bodies were buried at midnight and Sonny Dave Crowley performed the final farewell to his comrades in arms firing three revolver shots over the graves

There was one man who escaped from the ambush. His name was Cecil Guthrie he was the driver of the crossley tender no 2. He was later captured and shot and secretly buried in Annahala bog.

Connie O' Riordan (my Grandad) and I at the burial grounds in Castletown Kennagh

The site where Cecil was shot.

The bog where Cecil was secretly burried

Nell Kelly's house burned after ambush

The Kelly house of today

The Kelly family gathered their belongings and buried them in a trunk in a local bog.

After the Auxiliaries removed the dead and injured, O'Donoghues house was set alight. They then went to Nell Kelly's house and allowed Timothy time to remove his tools as this was his means of income, before setting this house alight also.

The Auxiliaries then went to Timmy Murray's house. Mrs Murray begged them not to burn the house as she was a widow with young children. They demanded a horse which she gave them. The horse later turned uninjured.

Eoin Hurley
Scoil Phádraig Naofa, Dunmanway.

The Kelly Family fled to Buttimers house Gothroe for the night. As Nell was running away she lost one of her confirmation shoes. The Kelly family were taken in by local families until their house was rebuilt in 1921. A grant was paid to rebuild the house Mikey Kelly's son's still reside in this house today.

Nell Kelly standing in the back
also in this photo Nell's mother, grandmother and siblings
This photo was taken around the time of the ambush.

Sore feet

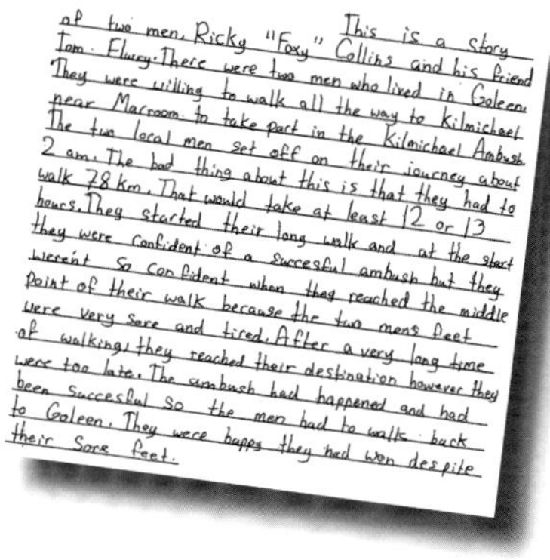

Áine Méabdh O'Regan
Scoil Mhuire National School, Schull.

[Handwritten version of the story text shown]

'This is a story of two men, Ricky "Foxy" Collins and his friend Tom Flurry … who lived in Goleen. They were willing to walk all the way to Kilmichael near Macroom to take part in the Kilmichael Ambush. The two local men set off on their journey about 2am. The bad thing about this is that they had to walk 78km. That would take at least 12 or 13 hours … after a very long time of walking, they reached their destination however they were too late. The ambush had happened and had been successful so the men had to walk back to Goleen. They were happy they had won despite their sore feet.'

Gave him a shotgun

Early that morning Tadgh Hurley known as "Leather" a travelling man was staying in a safe house nearby and was passing by the site. The Colum took him into the rocks and between the furs. They gave him a shotgun and gave him their plan.

When the fight was over Tom Barry said to Tadgh Hurley "You shot the biggest Devil in the Lorry". The travelling man pleased with his day continued his journey and enjoyed telling his story to the locals.

Laura Deasy
S.N Rath A' Bharraigh/Rathbarry National School.

Cart to coffin

HORSE & CART

Claire & Ella Dromey
Dromleigh National School.

A while before the Ambush, our great-grandad asked the local blacksmith to make him a cart for his farm. A few days later, the Ambush happened and sadly, three Irish men died. Since they didn't know that this was going to happen, they didn't have any timber to make the coffins. So, they used the timber supposed to be for our great-grandad's cart, to make the coffins!

The three men were taken to a house in gorthrue, one of the men were still alive but died in the women of the house's lap. John O' Coakley brought 3 coffins in a horse and cart for the men. The Local IRA men and neighbours then brought the 3 coffins in 3 horse drawn carts down Ahakerra, through Aherlick and as they were at Ballyvone cross there was a torch Light shone down on them, they thought is was the Tans but nothing happened. They carried the coffins by foot from chambers which is less then a mile from Castletown So they could jump over the ditch with the coffins if the Tans came. This was 1 or 2 am in the morning they could not bury the men in day light as the Tans would have been around the area. They were burried in Castletown by Cannon O' Connell from Enniskeane. The confession of all the column had been heard the night before in a house in Ahalana in o' Sullivans house.

Katie Scannell
St Joseph's GNS, Skibbereen.

Pointing their guns

'The auxiliaries came looking to Katie's mother for a horse and cart to bring out the bodies from the bog. Katie's brother Timothy had to stand on the haggard wall to tackle the horse as the auxiliaries were putting on the tackling upside down. They were pointing their guns as Timmy tackled the horse. To send the horse back home afterwards, they fired bullets on the ground.'

Shauna Lordan
St Mary's Senior School, Dunmanway.

'My great-granduncle Mikey's wife took a "bucket of tae" up to the flying column as they lay in wait for the Black and Tans in Kilmichael … after the ambush, on their way to their camp in Granure, they marched through my grandmother Noreen's homeplace in Balteenbrack where my great-granduncle met them in the dark.'

Ben Coughlan
Drimoleague National School.

Hid her dress under a rock

'My great grandmother's 9th birthday was on the same day as the ambush. Her Mam had given her a lovely dress for her birthday. She was afraid that the Black and Tans would burn down their house so she hid her dress in a nearby field underneath a rock. As it happens, the Black and Tans did call to their house, however, because her mother was a widow, she pleaded with them not to "burn the house" and they didn't.'

| Shauna Lordan
| St Mary's Senior School, Dunmanway.

Lost her confirmation shoe

Over the next few days there was major consequences for the people around the area.   Nell was quickly moved to a cottage in Shanacashel for safe keeping.   The familys urgency to move was very fast.   they had to run as fast as they could, Nell lost her shoe on the way and wasnt allowed back. Connie said till her dying day she would say that as a result of the Kilmichael ambush she had lost her good confirmation shoe.

| Lucia Duarte
| Dromleigh National School.

Tree riddled with bullets

The four days before the ambush the Column stayed at my grandmother's home place in Ahilnane near Enniskeane. They cleaned and oiled their guns on the kithen table and the oil is still to be seen on the table. They used a large tree behind the house as target practice and and years later when a storm knocked the tree down they couldn't cut it up with all the bullets in it.

| Patrick Collins
| Ballinacarriga National School.

| Shauna Lordan
| St Mary's Senior School, Dunmanway.

Saoirse Horgan
St Joseph's National School, Dromore.

Live like nothing ever happened

'My granny's mother is first cousins with Jim O'Sullivan … When he died his family had to pretend he was still alive because the Black and Tans were after them. My granny said "they had to live like nothing ever happened" … Jim was the only one that died on the site [of the ambush]. Jim is buried in Castletownkenneigh with Pat Deasy and Michael McCarthy. They put them in the bog … they moved them from the bog to Castletownkenneigh, they were buried in coffins and brought in a cart.'

Leah Kearney
St Mary's Senior School, Dunmanway.

Forced to walk

'My great great grandad was called Edward Dullea. He lived in Ballinacarriga. On a dark night when the Column were returning from Kilmichael on their way to the Faraway Camp of Granure, the Irish army made him march up the railway bridge at Manch and also the Bandon river bridge. They made him walk over the bridges to make sure there were no 'Tans about.'

Jason Howard
Ballinacarriga National School.

Put a bullet in it

Ciara O'Driscoll
Ballinacarriga National School.

When Con came home, back to the Far Away Camp, he came to get his horse and trap. He was sent to Kilbree near Clonakilty to collect Charlie Hurley who was the Brigade Commander. On the journey they heard a chain rattling on the road ahead of them. Con got off the trap to investigate the sound. Charlie warned him to take a gun and put a bullet in it. The sound turned out to be two goats tied together with a chain!

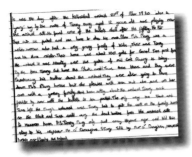

Andrew Scannell
St Patrick's BNS, Skibbereen.

'It was the day after the Kilmichael Ambush, the 21st of November 1920, a young boy by the name of Timmy Murry, aged 12 years old, was playing near the ambush site. He found some of the bullet shells after the fighting. He put them in his pocket and run home to show his mam. Now Mrs Murry was a widow woman who had a very young family of kids, there was Timmy and his three sisters. Their home was about 100 yards from General Tom's post for the ambush. It is exactly where the gates of mid-Cork quarries are today.

By the time Timmy got home the Black and Tans were there and they were questioning his mother about the ambush. They were also going to burn down Mrs Murry's house but she pleaded with them that she was on her own with a young family, and knew nothing about the ambush. Timmy was frightened by now with the bullets in his pocket. The only way the Black and Tans left the Murrys unharmed was Timmy had to put the cart on the family's horse so that the Black and Tans could carry the dead bodies from the ambush site to Macroom town. PS Timmy only passed away 10 years ago and told this story to his neighbour Mrs O'Donoghue.'

Ambush caused great trauma

Kathy rarely wanted to talk of the Kilmichael Ambush as it caused great trauma to all involed. They were so traumatised and upset to see bodies lying dead on the road, despite the fact they were the enemy. And of course they were heart broken to see their 3 friends shot dead. Kathy and her family witnessed their trauma and they needed much consoling. They were devastated.

Anna Goyal
St Joseph's Girls National School, Clonakilty.

Aoife Barry
St Mary's Senior School, Dunmanway.

Leaving their homes

'The day after the ambush people were leaving their homes to escape being burnt. One woman you could only see her legs underneath her tic (mattress, really a bag of flour stuffed with straw, rushes or feathers).'

Cillian & Eamon Cronin
Dromleigh National School.

Could see if any house on fire

Ciara Bradley
Dromleigh National School.

After the ambush all the local men stayed away from their homes at night in case they would be arrested. My greatgrandad Micheal is said to have stayed close to home and sheltered in the friends. But he may also have spent some (this) time in Kilnamartyra as his wife's family were from there and the story goes that a lot of Kilmichael men did that because it was high up over Kilmichael and they could see if any house was on fire.

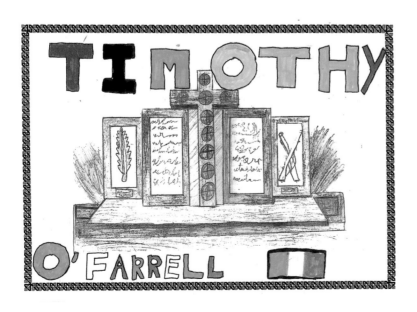

Orlaith Hickey
St Mary's Senior School, Dunmanway.

Little dog lying near body

Days after ambush the Tans wanted Conon Magnier of Dunmanway to ring the church bell as a mark of respect for the dead Tans but he refused and they boated that they would get the little man "with the red button." Some days later they shot Conon Magnier another man by the roadside and threw his body up on the ditch. When his body was found his little dog was lying beside him on the ditch. Some year later, back in my grandmoter's homeplace. Conon O Connell returned to Attend a station mass. On entry to the house he remarked " The last time I was in this house it was all guns, guns and guns "

Patrick Collins
Ballinacarriga National School.

Alice Barrett
Scoil Naomh Seosamh, Laragh.

Home Of John and Sarah Murphy

Éabha Murphy
Scoil Eoin National School, Innishannon.

Gunfire in Upton

On 15th February 1921, a train arrived at the Upton railway station full of British soldiers. The IRA started to shoot at the train and ambush the British soldiers. Fire then broke out as the British soldiers shot back. There were many innocent civilians, some of which were shot in crossfire. The civilians lay dead everywhere. The Ambush only lasted 10 minuets, but a lot were injured and killed including the driver, travellers and the ticket collector. Two IRA men were shot by the British soldiers and lay dead on the ground. A chase then broke out all over Upton and even beyond. One Ambusher was injured as he had been shot on the leg, but managed to escape from all the madness. Although he ran, he was limping and was being chased by the black and tans. He ran up my great-grandfathers fields until he reached my great-grandparents house at the top of Highfort hill. He knocked on the door very weakly as he was worried and tired. John and Sarah Murphy were upstairs hiding from all the noise but answered the door as soon as they realized that he wasn't part of the British troop. They hid him in a shed behind their house and bolted the door shut. They then hid Upstairs again, just as the black and tans arrived banging on their door. When John and Sarah answered the door, The two men questioned them. John and Sarah said that they did not know of anyone running around the area. In saying this, the black and tans were furious and shot bullets at the walls of their house. John and Sarah were quite unsure of the two, who then started raiding their house.

When they eventually left, John and Sarah brought the man in and dressed his wound. He rested until his leg was fit to walk on, and was sent on his way. He passed the gateway house at the end of the hill and also witnessed a lot of awful damages everywhere, but continued his voyage to get to a safe place.

'On the day my great, grandad was having his breakfast and an IRA soldier came in and said we need you to fight at the railway and he said "can I finish my breakfast first" and he finished his breakfast fast and went down to the Upton railway. And when the fighting broke out the IRA were out-numbered and then they said take cover. My great-grandad ran back home on the railway track and hid his gun. The next day he went to get his gun but it wasn't there so then he knew he had been followed.'

Diarmuid Brady
Scoil Eoin National School, Innishannon.

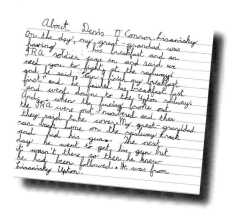

Billy Cronin
Scoil Mhaoilíosa, Knockavilla.

A really rough time

Con Sullivan fought in Upton where he got injured in the foot. He hid in my granda's house, for a while but the Black And Tans kept an eye on the house. Then the bullet went through the window. A few times they raided the house and broke the furniture etc but my great Granda and Gran uncle fled just in time, running in their night clothes and hid in the fields or under rock up in the nearby hills. It was a really rough time for them, fighting for their rights.

Natasha O'Donoghue
Drimoleague National School.

This is the monument next to the Upton railway station. As you can see it is a Celtic Cross. This monument is very old it has been there for ~~various~~ ages. The railway station is also very old but since the ambush they got new walls and plastered up the old walls

| Suzie Murphy
| Scoil Eoin National School, Innishannon.

Makes you wonder

This story saddened me to think innocent people had died. Today as I walk out the front door of the pub I look to my right where the memorial of the 1921 ambush was opened in 1968.

Only three of the 11 people that were killed were remembered on this monument – makes you wonder about the other innocent civilians who were killed on that day going about their normal daily tasks.

| Fiona Twohig
| Scoil Mhaoilíosa, Knockavilla.

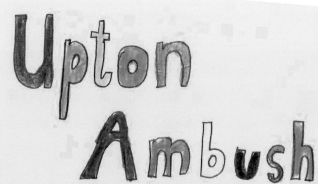

Wedding cake for condemned man

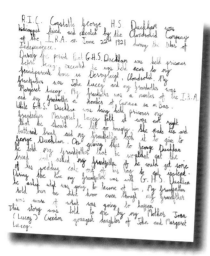

Muireann Kerry
Dromleigh National School.

'RIC Constable HS Duckham was kidnapped, tried and executed by the Clondrohid Company of the IRA on June 22nd 1921 during the War of Independence.

During the period while GHS Duckham was held prisoner before being executed, he was held near my grandparents' home in Derryleigh, Clondrohid … My grandfather was a member of the IRA and my grandmother a member of Cumann na mBan. While GHS Duckham was being held prisoner, my grandmother Margaret Lucey felt it was not right that he should be left go hungry. She made tea and buttered bread and my grandfather took it to give to George Duckham. On giving this to George Duckham, he told my grandfather that he wouldn't eat the bread but asked my grandfather if he could get some of his wedding cake out of his bag to eat instead. During the time my grandfather was with GHS Duckham he asked what was going to become of him. My grandfather told him he didn't know even though my grandfather was aware of what was going to happen.'

House burnt by RIC

'A man called John Sullivan and his brother James lived in their tall, newly painted houses at the eastern side of the village. The houses were on the right hand side as you travel towards Dunmanway. They were two different houses under one roof. On the night of 29th of September 1920 their houses were set on fire by uniformed men from the local police barracks. James was out of the house that night and John made an attempt to put out the fire but was prevented from doing so by the two policemen. He started to run from the house with his cash-box and books (he had a shop in that house) but they were taken from him by force and were thrown into the fire. John did not belong to any political organisation, his wife and nine children ran out of the house to escape the fire.'

Vincent Keane
Drimoleague National School.

This is a story about one of my cousins who was born at the turn of the last century in county Westmeath. His name was Andy Dolan. Andy was born into a poor Irish family. His father worked at a farm hand and he had 16 siblings. Four other sibliger didn't survive beyond child birth. Andy left school aged 12 but couldn't find a job. When he was old enough he went to work for the R.I.C (Royal Irish Constabulary) Andy eventually left the R.I.C when the I.R.A. (Irish Republican Army) threatened to shoot serving members. He felt afraid, almost terrified before he ended up in London. Andy attempted to join the British Army but returned to his hometown after getting nowhere. When he returned to his hometown he was rejected by the community because he worked for the R.I.C. He felt depressed and terribly sad. He died in isolation as an alcoholic several years later. He died in 1977.

'This is a story about one of my cousins who was born at the turn of the last century in County Westmeath. His name was Andy Dolan. Andy was born into a poor Irish family. His father worked as a farm hand and he had 16 siblings. Four other siblings didn't survive beyond childbirth. Andy left school aged 12 but couldn't find a job. When he was old enough he went to work for the RIC (Royal Irish Constabulary). Andy eventually left the RIC when the IRA (Irish Republican Army) threatened to shoot serving members. He felt afraid, almost terrified before he ended up in London. Andy attempted to join the British Army but returned to his hometown after getting nowhere. When he returned to his hometown he was rejected by his community because he worked for the RIC. He felt depressed and terribly sad. He died in isolation as an alcoholic several years later. He died in 1977.'

Louis Dolan Anderson
Scoil Mhuire National School, Schull.

Left Ireland

My great grandmother Eileen Melia was born in kilkenny 1905. She had lots of brothers and sisters. Her dad was a police man in the Royal Irish Constabulary. This was the time when Ireland was fighting for independence from England. Working for the police was dangerous and some people in the community were against them. My great grandmother was sent to England in 1916 to go to a boarding school in Leeds to get away from the fighting. In the years during the Civil War her whole family moved to England to get away from the war.

Kiva Scannell
Scoil Mhuire National School, Schull.

Revolver to his head

Raonaid Kerrisk
Leap National School.

John Browne: John Browne was an RIC man who was living in County Clare. He has a niece called Sheila Healy (living in Main Street, Leap.) John's mother, who was from Leap, owned a shop in Leap. The Black and Tans bought their cigarettes in her shop. The local IRA were fearful that Mrs Browne was passing on information to John, as he was an RIC man.

For that reason, at the age of 24, John Browne was shot by the IRA. He is buried in Leap Graveyard.

• John's brother, Tom, had a revolver (type of gun) put to his head and was threatened. He was told to leave Leap and never come back. He never returned! Tom also lived in Leap. •

My names is Killian Power. My great-great grandfather's name was Edmond Power. He was born in 1876 in Clashmore, Waterford and died in 1955 in Manchester. He became an R.I.C constable from 1897. Later he was promoted to sergeant in Co. Clare.

At times Edmond was in the same house as George O' Dwyer (quite an active I.R.A fighter in Kilkenny) but they were both on opposite sides of the war. They were very similar men. They were both Irish Catholics and also came from a farming background. It seems like they may have had an unspoken agreement not to snitch about each other's plans. Though their objectives would have been to kill each other or in Edmonds case; to arrest George. Edmonds son later lived with George and his wife. He didn't like them very much. This shows the complication of Irish families during the war of independence.

Killian Power
Scoil Mhuire National School, Schull.

George later became a chief superintendent in An Garda Siochana (pictured on the left)

Edmond later became a small farmer. He later moved to Manchester where he died in 1955

'None of my ancestors were directly affected by the 1916 Rising at that time … However, the aftermath of the Rising – [the] Civil War was brutal on Irish families. After [the] signing of the treaty in the Civil War brother fought against brother and cousin fought against cousin in some families. My great great grandad PJ O'Sullivan was one son of two and he lived out in Smithfield – out Union Hall road. [He] fought against his second cousin Diarmuid O'Donovan who lived out in Raheen Cross for years and years until PJ O'Sullivan's daughters that were nuns came back from Australia in 1965 and healed the rift. In the early '70s Smithfield was renovated and they found some guns from the Civil War. The guns were given to the Garda Station and my grandad Peter O'Sullivan asked for the guns, and even though there were no bullets inside the guns, he had to have a gun permit to have them. So my grandad … got a gun permit but he never got the guns in the end.'

Ailíse O'Sullivan
Gaelscoil Dhochtúir Uí Shúilleabháin, An Sciobairín.

Good people on both sides

I also had two Great Grand Uncles Séan and Andy Kelleher from Inniscarra who were bomb makers in The Rising. These brothers sadly ended up on opposite sides during the Civil war. One supported DeValera and one supported Michael Collins. My Granny said this happened a lot in families during the Civil War. She said there were good people on both sides.

Liam Henry Kearney
Scoil Phádraig Naofa, Dunmanway.

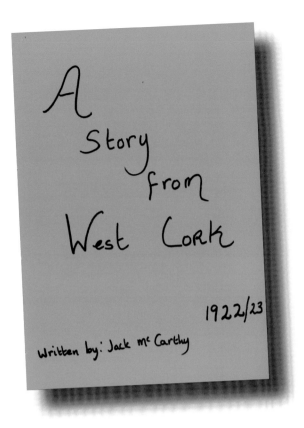

'Jimmy McCarthy was my great granduncle and he supported the free state under fine gael and that made him a "blueshirt". His neighbour, Ger O'Shea, supported De Valera, which meant he supported Fianna Fáil and the Irish Republican Army (IRA). They believed that Michael Collins should not have agreed to 26 counties but all 32 only.

Jimmy's house was a safe house where another neighbour used to hide from Ger O'Shea. Jimmy was a tall strong man. Once when a neighbour was hiding in my great granduncle's house, Ger O'Shea came to the door. He demanded that the neighbour hiding there should round up his best bullock for slaughtering to feed the IRA. At this time, this was a form of punishment. If it was not done, Ger O'Shea and his men threatened to shoot the man. My great granduncle Jimmy McCarthy came to the door and spread his arms wide saying "no man will pass me" to stop Ger O'Shea entering to take away the other neighbour. Ger O'Shea stuck the hay pike he was holding through Jimmy's hand. Ger O'Shea left the house after that and Jimmy's neighbour was saved that night from the IRA.'

Jack McCarthy
Scoil Eoin National School, Innishannon.

Not allowed to see mother

My Granny mrs Noreen Collins from Morahin. Her dad was not allowed to see his mother in her own house because of politics. My grandfather could only see his mother in the sisters house because the brother lived with the mother and could not go in because they would have a fight about Michael Collins and Eamon De valera. So the mother had to go across the road to the sisters house to see her son and daughter

Maebh Collins
Kilcoe National School.

Wife bans Free State Uniform

My great great grandfather on my grandmothers side of the family even is the Free State Army and his wife even an I.R.A supporter. He wouldn't let him in without taking his uniform off first.

Byron O'Sullivan
Abbeystrewry National School, Skibbereen.

America or Spike Island

He later joined the Republican side in the Civil war. He had to Immigrate to America when De Valera and his followers got beat. It was either America or Spike Island and he went to America. He had to stay in America from 1923 until 1937. He came back when De Valera got into power.

Michael Collins
Drimoleague National School.

To America

Saoirse Horgan
St Joseph's National School, Dromore.

At the time the Irish Civil War had started (June 1922/May 1923) and Irishmen were fighting each other. One side wanted independence, the other didn't – it was a sad cruel war.

'At the time that the Irish civil war had started (June 1922/May 1923) and Irishmen were fighting each other. One side wanted independence, the other didn't – it was a sad cruel war.
A ship belonging to the Free State forces, "the Muirchú", was sailing up the harbour with its guns ready. Some anti-Treaty soldiers were thought to be in the woods above Courtmacsherry, so the guns were fired across the harbour. Everyone was terrified. A bullet hit the window sill of my grandad's house and the hole is still there. My great grandfather and his baby sister hid on the pier along with all the other frightened people. He told my granny that the Treaty men escaped and nobody was injured or killed. It was a very sad time in Ireland in those days.'

Cormac O'Flynn
Scoil Naomh Seosamh, Laragh.

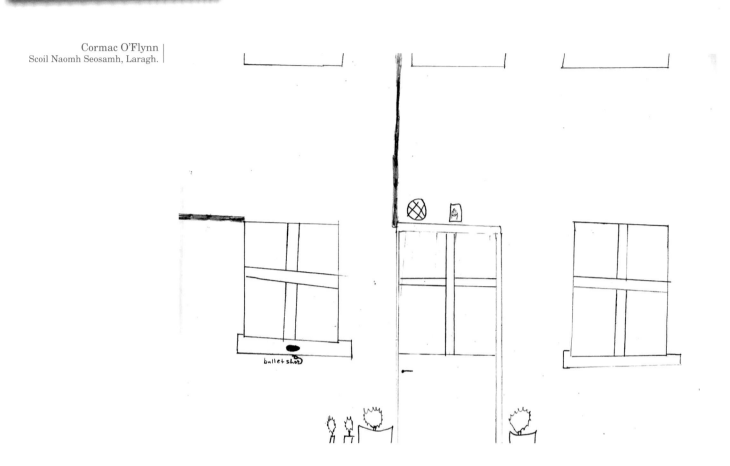

Snipers on [St] Patrick's Street

'He was a student in the de la Salle College, Waterford, during the Civil War. When returning to college in January 1923, he got the train from Drimoleague to Cork, as usual, planning to get a further train to Waterford. However, the railway lines were cut and he was forced to stay in the Victoria Hotel in Cork overnight. The hotel staff instructed the guests to sleep in the corridors as there were gunfights/ snipers on Patrick's St and there was a danger of being shot through the windows if they stayed in the bedrooms. On the following day he had to travel to Waterford on a trawler – the trawlerman was conducting a "ferry" service as roads and railways were cut.'

Eoin O'Sullivan
St Patrick's BNS, Skibbereen.

William Kelly

out part of a carpenter's mallet. During the Civil War, he supported the Anti-Treaty side. He was captured along with a friend of his Denis Lucey from Kilnamatra, ... while ... they were on active duty in New Ross on 13th August 1922.

He was imprisoned in the Curragh, Co. Kildare. His brother Michael Kelly cycled from Dunmanway to visit him in prison. Michael was not allowed to see his brother and returned home. About half-way down from Kildare, he received news of William's death in the Curragh. William died on the 15th April 1923. He was 27 years old. Later on, his family found out that William had been taken out by two Free State Officers and told to swear an oath of allegiance to the Free State, but he had refused, replying "Death before dishonour", and he had been bayonetted. He died a short time later, and the family believed it was a result of the wounds he had received for not swearing the oath and for his refusal to sign a statement declaring he would not take up arms: they did not believe the cause of death, as officially given, was ill health.

'During the Civil War [William Kelly] supported the anti-treaty side. He was captured along with a friend of his Denis Lucey from Kilnamatra, while they were on active duty in New Ross on 13th August 1922. He was imprisoned in the Curragh, Co. Kildare. His brother Michael Kelly cycled from Dunmanway to visit him in prison. Michael was not allowed to see his brother and returned home. About half way down from Kildare, he received news of William's death in the Curragh. William died on the 15th of April 1923. He was 27 years old. Later on his family found out that William had been taken out by two Free State Officers and told to swear an oath of allegiance to the Free State, but he refused, replying "Death before dishonour", and he had been bayonetted. He died a short time later, and the family believed it was a result of the wounds he had received for not swearing the oath ... they did not believe the cause of death, as officially given, was ill health.'

His Burial

'William's remains were brought to Cork city but, because of the Bishop's excommunication of IRA soldiers, no church would accept his remains. After a lot of argument with the church officials, my great-grandfather, Denis Kelly, who knew one of the priests personally, managed to have William's remains allowed into St Peter and Paul's church. However, this was conceded only on condition it would take place after 11 o'clock at night and that they would be gone before first light the following morning. William could have been buried in the Republican Plot in St Finbarr's cemetery but the family preferred a burial with family members in Kilmichael cemetery.'

Caoimhe Foley
Scoil Naomh Seosamh, Laragh.

William Kelly, Clogher, Dunmanway,
'G' Company, 1st Battlion, 1st Cork Brigade, IRA. Died 15/4/1923.

Seán Collins was Michael Collins older brother!
Jim Hurley was Seán age. They grew up together
and were the best of friends. But when Civil War
broke out the two friends, soon became enemies.
It was believed that Jim Hurley was part of Michaels
Collins ambush. After the war, Jim and Seán made up
and were best friends once more. The ultimate reconcilation
gesture was to be buried in ajoining graves despite what
had happened between them in the years together.
They are buried in St. Marys Cymetry in ajoining graves.
in Clonakilty.

Míscha May Pattwell |
St Joseph's Girls National School, Clonakilty. |

Shooting broke out between the mourners

Sarah Connolly |
Rathmore National School. |

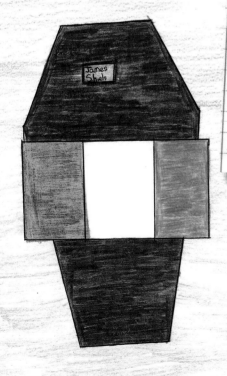

This is his coffin with
the Irish Flag over it

My great grand-uncle Michael O'Conell (Mikey) was
born in 1907 in Rathcooney in Glanmire just
outside Cork City. (See his home place marked on photo 1)
He died of cancer on 14th November, 1922, when he
was 15 years old. Mikey was buried in Rathcooney
cemetery, just down the road from his house.
His burial took place on 16th November, 1922. At the
same time that day, a soldier named John Francis
Cronin was being buried in the same cemetery.
He was a Free State Soldier and he was buried
in plot B2C2.
   While both burials were going on, shooting
broke out between the mourners of John Francis
Cronin and the Anti-Treaty supporters. This meant
that Mikey's family had to flee from the
cemetery, without filling in the grave. That night,
some neighbours returned to the cemetery to
fill in the grave, after dark.

Caoimhe Shiels |
Dromleigh National School. |

Broke her neck

After the War of Independence there was a split of the I.R.A. when people either took the Republican side or became members of the 'Free state' army; the Irish Civil War happened because of that split. My great Grandfather, Andrew, took the Republican side.

As a result of this, my great Grandfather had a very sad experience. He was made a prisoner of the 'Free State Army' because he was opposed to their ideas. He was in jail in the building that we now know as St Fachtna's de la Salle in Skibbereen. On the 30th of September 1922, his mother Kate Mac Carthy, was travelling home from Skibbereen in her donkey and cart. It seems she looked up to the jail to try to get a glimpse of her son. There were barricades lining the street and as she looked up, she lost control of the donkey and fell out of the cart. She broke her neck and died as a result. My great Grandfather was then released from his imprisonment but had to suffer the loss of his mother.

Alannah Crowley
Caheragh National School.

Nightmares about sides

1916-1923

Willie didn't have a gun during the war but after the truce, he discovered he was a crack shot and became a sniper during the Civil War where he fought on the Anti Treaty side. Willie became Captain of the Ballineen Company 4th Battalion Cork number 3 Brigade. His brother Con was the Company Quarter Master.

Willie's Son Liam tells me he remembers his father been given a shotgun once as an older man in his mid sixties and he shot 2 crows in seconds flat. He said he was West Cork Darts champion several times proving what a great eye he had.

like a lot of people who have witnessed armed combat, Willie didn't speak a lot about his involvement and Liam says that his dad had nightmares about sides during those times nearly a hundred years ago. When Willie died in   He was given a military guard of honour as a tribute to the part he played during those times at the birth of our Nation.

Ar dheis Dé go raibh a anam.

Ronan Crowley
Scoil Phádraig Naofa, Bandon.

Bullet holes in hat

Ava

Mo Shin-Sheannithir (17/11/2017)

Sceal fíor

During the Civil war, local Republican, Charles Dullea was on the wanted list of the Free State soldiers. At a threshing in McCarthys of Codnaconartha in Autumn of 1922, Dullea was helping to make the straw-rick when the free state soldiers appeared in search of him. Dullea was covered with straw by his friends and when one of the soldiers went up on the rick demanding to know his whereabouts, they replied that they had not seen him. At this the soldier fired a bullet from his rifle into the straw near the spot Dullea was hiding. The soldiers then left and after a long dramatic pause the tention was relieved when Dullea emerged from the straw. holding in his hand was his hat, wich had recieved two bullet holes from the bullet that just narrowly missed.

Níor mhaith le Charles na Sasraigh. Throid sé sa chogga neamhspleasach na hÉirinn. Le linn an cogadh domhan saighdiúrí státe saor ag long dó.

Ava Ní Throithigh |
Gaelscoil Dhroichead na Banndan. |

Never walked again

My Great-Great Grandfather William Timothy O' Connor was shot in both knees by The Free-State Army for being a member of the I.R.A and for storing guns for them. A couple weeks later he was shot in both knees at Acoose Lake, Killarney.

He never walked again and eventually had both legs from knee down amputated. My mom remembers him from when she was 4 or 5 years old, She used to call him Daddy Tim.

Isabella O'Sullivan |
Abbeystrewry National School, Skibbereen. |

When the War of Independence ended, he returned home to his farm.
He also fought in the civil war where he and the IRA were against the Anglo Irish Treaty.
During that time he signed his farm over to his sister beacause if he was captured again or shot the state would take all his possesions including his farm. A local man named Jonas Calnan worked the farm while he was away. In 1928 he got his farm back.

Emma O'Donovan
Caheragh National School.

'It was interesting how Michael was willing to talk about the history of times up to the split that came after the treaty. You could see that he was uncomfortable talking about the civil war that followed. Men started to disagree with each other within their own towns, villages and columns. Michael feels it was the downfall of the country. For so many years that followed and that so many intelligent and strategic men were killed by fellow countrymen when they should have continued to work together against a common enemy.'

Matthew Hoban
Scoil Mhaoilíosa, Knockavilla.

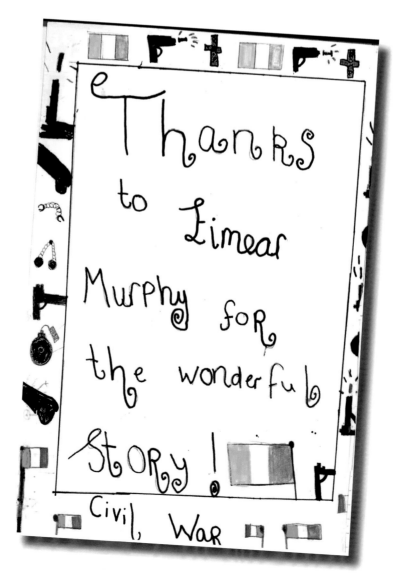

Sáorlaith Murphy
Dromleigh National School.

Chapter 11

PROTESTANT STORIES

These accounts reveal how Anglo Irish families, particularly those who supported the Crown forces, were targeted by the IRA for money and arms, with some executed as 'spies'. As potential billets for British forces, some 'big houses' were burnt, while others provided sanctuary to volunteers on the run.

Rachel Crowley
St Joseph's National School, Dromore.

William was born (1900) and reared in Kilbrittain, County Cork. The 1911 census shows William, age 11, living at number 7 house in Kilbrittain Town with his father Edward, mother Amelia and his brother and sisters. The youngest child in the house at the time was Ethel my great granny who was 2 and a half.

Families were very big at the time and William's family were no different. Here is an old family photo we are lucky to have:

William and his family were protestant and Edward, William's father, was a constable in the RIC.

The family were living in Kilbrittain at the time of the uprising and life became quite difficult for them because of their religion. There were constant threats at the time that all protestants in West Cork would be shot and there were lots of killings at the time.

Seamus Griffiths
Rathmore National School.

William Fitzell Blennerhasset Johnston was shot in Kilbrittain on 9 February 1921, and while no reason was given, the Cork Constitution believed it was the RIC connection (William was due to follow his father in to the RIC) along with his religion. Johnston was found with a bullet in the back of his head and a note on his body saying that he was a spy. It is believed he was shot dead by the IRA at his home.

Following the shooting Amelia applied for compensation and it was reported in The Skibbereen Eagle, the local newspaper of the time:

Amelia Johnston, widow, claimed compensation for the death of her son, William Johnston , aged 21 years , who was shot near Kilbrittain. Mr. J. F. Bourke, B.L. (instructed by Mr. J. Travers Wolfe) for the applicant. Mrs. Johnston stated that her son who was shot was an accepted candidate for the police. While out hunting rabbits, he was shot at Ballymore, one and a half miles from Kilbrittain. His Honor awarded £2000 to the widow and £200 each child.

This must have been a lot of money at the time!

The name of William Johnston appears in the Compensation Commission Register under 9 February 1921, with the notation that British liability was accepted, and with a note that £2,000 was awarded.

The events in 1921 would shape the history of my family and where they all lived in the future as you will now see.

The IRA raided the family home in October 1921. In the view of the RIC, this was done in order to intimidate Amelia and her children into leaving the area. They first moved to Bandon and then on to Donegal where they had family and where they felt safe.

William Johnston was buried next to his father Edward in Rathclarin burial ground near Kilbrittain.

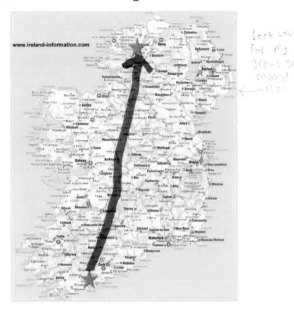

My great granny Ethel, who now lived in Donegal with her mother Amelia and brothers and sisters, met my great grandpa there who coincidentally was also a constable like her father Edward. She still had connections in County Cork as some of her older sisters had stayed there. My grandpa Joe was born and reared in the north of the country but always felt his heritage in West Cork.

Joe hated the division between Catholics and Protestants and when he was a young man he decided to leave all this behind and seek his fortune in South America! He was well educated and managed to secure a job as a commodity broker in Brazil. He set sail from Ireland to England and then onward to Brazil when he was only 20. Here is a copy of his immigration card:

My grandpa met my granny (the daughter of his boss) in Rio. She was an Anglo-Brazilian but more importantly a catholic and this did not go down well with my great granny Ethel who was still fearful of Catholics because of William being shot. This didn't stop my grandpa and he married my granny in 1959.

Grandpa Joe was very interested in Education and decided that the best place for his children to go to school was England so he moved his wife and 3 children to Oxfordshire in the South in 1968 and my mum, Dee, was born a few years later followed by my uncle Patrick. While my mum was a little girl my grandpa re-trained to be a teacher and spent the rest of his years until his retirement as a head teacher of a big boys school.

Even though my grandpa had been all over the world his favourite place was still West Cork and my mum spent all the summer holidays in the families holiday cottage just outside Skibbereen. When Grandpa retired from teaching all he wanted to do was to move back to Ireland and he and my granny did in 1990.

My mum Dee loves West Cork as much as my Grandpa and after she had trained as a teacher,

married my dad Jim and had my older brother Joseph, they too decided to move here. Myself and my younger sister were born and reared here and so finally the family has gone full circle.

The family has moved all over the place but the best place is West Cork!

Refusals from 'big houses'

'The local volunteers of the West Cork Brigade took up Arms Funds Collections in October 1919. They met with a lot of refusals in particular from the people who lived in "big houses". On foot of these refusals, it was decided that 22 cattle would be taken in ones and twos from these people when a market had been found for them … The reprisals came fast and furious with RIC and British Military raiding suspects' homes and going as far as burning Neiluis Connolly's home in Coolnagurrane to the ground in March 1920.'

Aisling Collins
St Joseph's GNS, Skibbereen.

1919 ○ He collected money for the arms fund.

○ He also collected arms and ammunition mainly from the prodestant community some by force, some without force.

Ellie McCarthy
St Joseph's GNS, Skibbereen.

Protestant farmers shot

Protestant farmers shot near Skibbereen

Sometime around 1916-1917, two Protestant farmers from Lissanoohig, north of the Abbey in Skibbereen, were shot by the IRA.

At that time, the IRA were collecting money for funds. Two big farmers, Sweetman and Connell, not only refused to pay up but they also reported the fundraising efforts back to the RIC (Royal Irish Constabulary). The two men were taken out of their homes one night and shot.

The man who killed them is known. He was not a West Cork man. The families left the area and the farms were auctioned.

Ciara Nic Cormaic
Gaelscoil Dhochtúir Uí Shúilleabháin, An Sciobairín.

'There were two Church of Ireland gentlemen shot dead sometime between 1920-21 in the townland of Lissanuhig in the parish of Skibbereen. They were shot by the local Column of the IRA volunteers because it was assumed that these two men were spies for the British establishment. Their names were Mr Matt Sweetman and Mr Bill Connell. These men were local farmers and apparently had no involvement in the local activities, only that it was rumoured that Mr Sweetman's daughter was involved with a British soldier from the local 6th British Regiment. They left behind wives and children.'

Kate Hurley
Lisheen National School.

‘Our house is called Kilcoman Park House … In 1919 the Lamb family lived in our house … Because they were an Anglo/Irish family the IRA were going to burn it down. Mary's brother Fred Dobbin was a doctor and he lived with them during the first world war. Fred had treated both the IRA and the Black and Tans. After a while both sides agreed that it should not be burnt down as he was a doctor each side could go and see.'

Sam & Ben Jones |
Kilcolman National School. |

The Burning of Speight's big house in Union Hall

The Leap cumman of the IRA raided and burnt down Speight's house around 1918. Speight was a retired Colonel of the British Army. He had a big house in Union Hall and also owned the RIC barracks in Leap. The IRA didn't have anything against Speight himself so he wasn't harmed.

Before burning the house, the IRA spent 3 days and 3 nights drawing stuff out of the house and it was all taken away by the IRA members. A lot of the items ended up in houses in West Cork: a piano, a door, cutlery, binoculars, a clock. Some people know the location of some of these items which are in local houses to this day. Some very valuable furniture is in a house in Ardfield.

There was a Catholic 'Stations' in Donal (Danlo) O'Donovan's house in Ballyroe. After Mass, when breakfast was served with cutlery engraved with 'Speight', a man refused to join in the meal until the cutlery was removed.

A local rhyme:

"Can anybody tell me where did Speights piano go?

Maybe up to Cullenagh or down to Ballyroe

But can anybody tell me where did Speight's piano go?"

After that, Speight's piano was advertised for sale at many local auctions, it was used as a means to attract a bigger crowd. The piano never turned up at the auctions, having been sold on in private.

The people who took the house contents never had any luck after that.

Ciara Nic Cormaic |
Gaelscoil Dhochtúir Uí Shúilleabháin, An Sciobairín. |

Speight's piano

Rachel Crowley |
St Joseph's National School, Dromore. |

‘Colonel William F. Speight and his wife Lucy … owned a mansion with 24 rooms in Union Hall village. They also were the owners of the building in Leap that served as the local Police Barracks.
The local IRA burned down his house. Before they had burned it down, they raided his house so they would have all of his goods. Seemingly anyone who acquired contents from Speight's house would never have good luck!'

Raonaid Kerrisk |
Leap National School. |

At the time my Great Grandfather, Reginald Perrott was living at Little Silver, Bandon, just a few miles from Upton. Following the attack two men came into the yard on their way to a safe house across the river. One was injured badly and the other almost carried him. They asked Reginald to hide them. This he did. When an army patrol pulled into the place he said he'd seen no one out of the ordinary. Once the patrol passed they went on their way again. Because of this, word went out that the family were now protected by the IRA and they were not affected by the Bandon Valley Murder of 13 protestants in 1922.

Zara Stout
The Model School, Dunmanway.

Carly Helbrow
Ballinadee National School.

One night, in Cork city there was a soldier madly knocking at every door in sight, hoping that somebody would let him inside, for the army were after him. But no one would let him in because they were scared of being caught. In one of the houses there was a woman looking out of a window.

The soldier didn't knock at this door because it was a protestant house and he did not expect to be let in, but the woman looking out of the window opened the door and gestured him inside her house. She hid him up in the attic and when the army came they checked every house apart from the woman's house because it was a protestant and they thought that the soldier wouldn't be let inside. So the woman fed the soldier and healed him and in a couple of days he was ready to leave.

'The British were after a priest to kill him. He went into a Protestant house to hide from them. He hid under the floorboards. They left him out every night and took care of him ... When it was over he went back to his house and he said "I have no money to give you but I will give you my blessing that you will never have no money", and to this day they still have lots of money!'

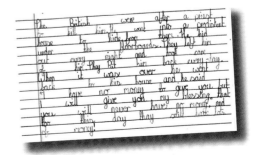

Hazel Deane
Abbeystrewry National School, Skibbereen.

They said that the people in our family from 1916 to 1923 were Nelson Roycroft and his wife Doris (nee Nealon). They travelled to Canada in 1921. A lot of my family, being of church of Ireland denomination, left Skibbereen during this period.

Oran Roycroft |
Abbeystrewry National School, Skibbereen. |

They may have had a different attitude to British authority in Ireland however, because all through the troubles the Hosford yard was freely used by their workman for drilling IRA members. Protestant homes were less likely to be raided by the Black and Tans because they were thought to be more law abiding.

Many of that family emigrated, as did a lot of protestant people (about 60,000) around this time. They felt vulnerable, living in West Cork. While not many were actively involved in republican activity they turned a blind eye to it, whether through nationalistic beliefs, fear of the rebels or loyalty to neighbours on the run, I don't know.

Zara Stout |
The Model School, Dunmanway. |

We don't know when Robert joined up but it must have been towards the end of the war. It seems that he suffered badly from shell shock and was sent home from the war with a brown paper tag on him, like a luggage label. He didn't speak for a while and had terrible nightmares.

While he had been away the family had let out the post office to someone else and in the changed atmosphere in Ireland at the time he was told that he'd now forfeited the licence to run the post office. He was unable to concentrate to continue his studies as a vet and having been demobbed a couple of days short of any entitlement to an army pension he suffered at all hands!

His grandparents couldn't cope with him, so he was sent to live with cousins called Roycroft, who lived in Ballydehob, County Cork. This family had a small farm but no sons to take on all the work. Robert did recover in time and went on to marry his cousin Sadie Nixon and run the family farm in West Cork.

At some stage, on his return to Ireland, IRA members came to the house demanding his old British army uniform. He told them that he didn't have it any longer though they put a gun to his chest. An unmarried aunt intervened and the gun was not fired. He quietly burned it and his medal in a barrel afterwards so they couldn't ever get it. They did insist that he passed on his knowledge of fire arms to members of the IRA in the locality.

Zara Stout |
The Model School, Dunmanway. |

Darragh O'Regan
St Joseph's National School, Dromore.

Ashlee Madden
Scoil Eoin National School, Innishannon.

Chapter 12

REVOLUTION ABROAD

This period was one of revolution, insurgency and war internationally and here we have personal family accounts from Poland, Russia, Greece, Latvia, Spain and India.

Agata Kalkowska
St Mary's Senior School, Dunmanway.

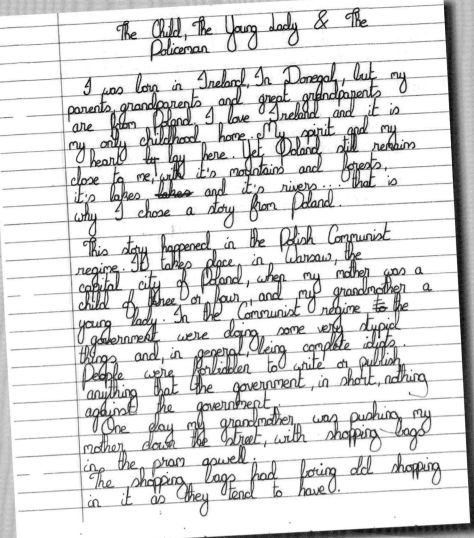

The Child, The Young Lady & The Policeman

I was born in Ireland, In Donegal, but my parents, grandparents and great grandparents are from Poland. I love Ireland and it is my only childhood home. My spirit and my heart lie by here. Yet Poland still remain close to me, with it's mountains and forests, it's lakes and it's rivers.... that is why I chose a story from Poland.

This story happened in the Polish Communist regime. It takes place, in Warsaw, the capital city of Poland, when my mother was a child of three or four, and my grandmother a young lady. In the Communist regime the government were doing some very stupid things and, in general, being complete idiots. People were forbidden to write or publish anything that the government, in short, nothing against the government.

One day my grandmother was pushing my mother down the street, with shopping bags in the pram as well. The shopping bags had boring old shopping in it as they tend to have.

But what has shopping got to do with Communist Regime in Poland?... You might well ask. laaaaaah! But you see, secret, newspapers and books were hidden in with the shopping.... You see my hr grandmother was somebody in the Communist-Regime to whom secret-papers were sent about all that was happining in Poland at that time. She passed them on to other people and sent on the news...

Now a policeman came along and as my grandmother was rather attracting (if you don't mind my saying so, he asked her if he could help her carry the shopping bags. Now being a very clever woman she agreed - pardon me about saying she's clever, but she is-...

That is a funny scene. A policeman carrying a shopping bag, not knowing that inside it are illegal papers.....

And he never found out... Funny, ain't it?!!

Lucija Kluzniak Madajczak
Abbeystrewry National School, Skibbereen.

INDIA UNDER BRITISH RULE

Ashan Waseem
St Joseph's National School, Dromore.

My Grandad's Answer

Shourya Malik
Scoil na mBuachaillí, Clonakilty

Gandhi was getting India's Independence
On the other side of the city my grandfather was living in a big apartment and about 21. Some British soldiers barged into every apartment looking for food. When they were in my grandfather's apartment they couldn't find anything because my grandad hid it so well.

After some time the soldiers left. My grandfather drove to his friend's house. He told him what happened and his friend was shocked that he could be next to be robbed so he told my grandfather about Gandhi. Later my grandad and his friend were in a car driving to Gandhi. They found him walking on the beach peacefully. My grandfather and his friend walked beside him and told him about the British soldiers taking their food. Gandhi's answer was to go on a fast and hide all the food.

All the neighbourhood hid their food in a box under the ground when my grandad and his friend told everyone. The British soldiers got really annoyed that they have to buy the food like normal people.
The End
(My uncle is a very dramatic person)

Stories of the Revolution.

My great-great grandfather, Dimitris, was involved as a soldier of the Greek army in two major historical events. The first was the Allied intervention of the Russian Civil War in 1919. After the Bolshevik government withdrew from World War One, the Allied powers (France, Britain, Italy, United States) openly backed the anti-communist White Forces in Russia. Dimitris, after a few years of training, and despite being only 18 years old, went to Crimea on a battleship and took part in the capture of the cities Odessa and Sevastopol. They held their positions for about six months and in spring 1919 were forced to leave after a strong Russian attack. Dimitris spent a few months in Constanza, Romania, where the Allies were re-grouped and then were sent to Smyrna/Izmir in Turkey as the Greco-Turkish war had just begun. He took part in many battles in Minor Asia where the Greek Army advanced and gained territory until 1921. Then, the Greek front collapsed and after a Turkish counter-attack, the war ended in 1922 with the the recapture and the great fire of Smyrna. Dimitris was lucky enough to survive

Realtín Deli
Gaelscoil Mhichíl Uí Choileáin, Clonakilty.

The Revolution of 1917

'The Revolution in 1917 brought drastic changes. By this time there were about 100 German prisoners of war in Melzani. Then sailors came from Moscow promising to kill the gentry and take possession of the estate. At first they received no help from the peasants who were relatively well off under the von Gabbes. But finally the peasants decided to take over the estate themselves. The Germans in the village got to know and warned us. We quickly prepared two charabancs (drawn by Orloff horses) and drove through the village before the peasants realised what was happening and then on to Saransk. Mr. von Gabbe had stayed behind to see what would happen. He arrived several days later in a complete state of shock. The estate, he said, had been divided among the peasants, the house plundered and then burned. There was nothing left'.

Hilde eventually found a transport repatriating German prisoners of war and so finally reached Hamburg in 1918.

Freya Scott
Gaelscoil Mhichíl Uí Choileáin, Clonakilty.

My great great grandad was in the Latvian War of independance. His name was Janis Cirulis he was born in August 1914 and died in 2005. After a few years he Participated in WW2 in a different Countri

In 1945 he came back to Latvia and had a peaceful Life after that

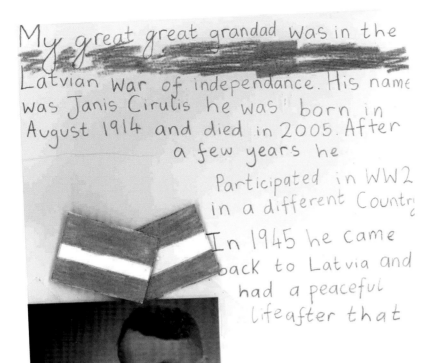

Liana Cirule
Kilgarriffe National School.

Executed in the woods

Lucy Bielecki
St Joseph's GNS, Skibbereen.

Jan Bielecki 1898 –1939

My Great Grandfather Jan Bielecki took part In one of the most important tank battles of the Early twentieth century. The Bolvesheviks. (under Lenin) meent to take over the newly reformed country of Poland and then the rest of Europe. They fought a Battle outside Warsaw. The Polish Army was not expected to win this battle but they did. Under the command of Andres and Skorsky, this meant that Europe DiD not become communist. Sadly when stanin took over from Lenin was when the second World War storted, and the men who served In that earlier Battle (including my Great Grandfather and His seven brothers) were taken off by the Russians and excecuted in katin woods.

| Agata Kalkowska
| St Mary's Senior School, Dunmanway.

! The full story !

It was the 11th of November 1918 in this day Poland not only won its independence but also it got back on the map. It got its independence from Germany Austria-Hungary and Russia. It started with Pitsudski being appointed commander chief by the RC *regency council*. He was entrusted with creating a national Goverment for the restored Polish state.

Most Germans were is Warsaw so it was easy for demonized Soldiers to disarmed them. They did the same to the Austrians and Russians

Spanish Civil War

| Marcal Kottler
| Scoil Bhríde National School, Ballydehob.

-My Great grandpa Josep Participated -in the Spanish civil war. He fought -against Franco (a spanish dictator). During -The war my granny Carme was born; -They had little food and drink In Spain -they spoke catalon but Franco didn't- -allow them. If he caught somebody -speaking catalon he would kill them. -My other great grandpa Predric, as he -was older and he was a builder he stayed -in the village and he dug a undergroun -basement. The catalon lost and the -spanish won.

Chapter 13

PS FROM THE KIDS

The children's essays repeatedly tell us how much they learnt
through their participation in this project. They clearly enjoyed
engaging with the older generation, gaining insights into their
ancestors' experience and the reality of war through their own
interpretation of events.

Lucija Kluzniak Madajczak
Abbeystrewry National School, Skibbereen.

I have never realised the amount of history that happened here in west Cork and going to Steve Lynch's house and hearing the facts and stories of what actually happened through those years was amazing. It was great to hear stories about my actual family, such as my great-grandmother who were so involved in the troubles of those years. They were involved in both of the stories I have written here and prominent figures of those times. Even though there were no lives lost in Ballydehob there are still many stories of fights and battles. And These figures that come before us helped pave the way to make a better life for us and all future familys here in West Cork to this day

I only loved working on this project and I am sad it is now over

'I have never realised the amount of history that happended here in West Cork and going to Steve Lynch's house and hearing the facts and stories about what actually happened through those years was amazing. It was great to hear stories about my actual family … And these figures that came before us helped pave the way to make a better life for us and all future families here in West Cork to this day. I truly loved working on this project and I am sad it's now over.'

Ellen O'Donovan
Scoil Bhríde National School, Ballydehob.

-I really enjoyed doing this project with my grandad (Connie O'Riordan). When he took me around the site I could picture it all in my head and understand it better.

I would like if local history could be taught in school as I found this very Intresting

My grandad and I at the Kilmichael monument (Nell Kelly's son)

Eoin Hurley
Scoil Phádraig Naofa, Dunmanway.

I have learnt so much from this project and read how so many poor innocent families suffered. We should all be kind to each other and be grateful that there is no war going on in Ireland today. Everyone in their own lives may be fighting their own hard battles but we should strive for peace and happiness in the world.

Molly Hilliard
Coppeen National School.

'Throughout my project I learned a lot … I enjoyed my time with my grandad, it's made me and him closer. I now regularly talk to him about events from our country and the greater world. I now regularly look up videos about history.'

Connor Collins
St Joseph's National School, Dromore.

Like the people of that generation, my Great-Grandfather was very reserved to talk about the war. Only for my Grandfather's love of history and the research he has done, my family would never know what happened on their doorstep during the War of Independence.

Claire Scanlon
Knockskeagh National School.

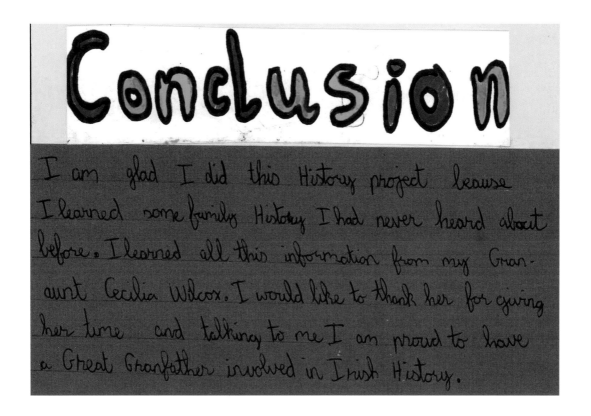

Conclusion

I am glad I did this History project because I learned some family History I had never heard about before. I learned all this information from my Gran-aunt Cecilia Wilcox. I would like to thank her for giving her time and talking to me I am proud to have a Great Granfather involved in Irish History.

Greg Mulhall
St Joseph's National School, Dromore.

Why I chose Michael O Driscoll

O O O a O O O

I chose Michael O'Driscoll because he is my great-grandad. He is my granny's father and she told me all about him and his achievments. I am very truly proud that my great-grandad was part of Irelands amazing history.

Abbie McCarthy & Laura Dullea
St Mary's Senior School, Dunmanway.

Dan O Callaghan didn't fight in the civil war as he was arrested and imprisoned in Cork Jail for 1 year and for 2 more years in the Curragh county Kildare. While he was in Jail his brother Ned came home and ran the farm. When he was released he came home farming. His family say that he didn't speak much to them about the "troubles" but it was a terrible time but in his opinion it had to be done. We owe these people so much for fighting for our independence.

Pádraig Tobin
Ardagh Boy's National School.

An 80th year old hand, holding the bullet that my Grandmother picked up at My Great Grandads funeral.

Katie Scannell
St Joseph's GNS, Skibbereen.

I find this side of my family fascinating and it has prompted my granny to Refresh her memories by talking to her surviving relitivs before the information is gone for good

Tara O'Farrell
Scoil Eoin National School, Innishannon.

Gone to their graves with secrets

My Grandad told me that both my great Grandads would have been part of the local IRA & may have knocked the bridge that nyght back in November 1920 & he told me that it is a distinct possibility that great Grandads of some of my classmates may have been some of the men who had shots fired at them but all those men who have now gone to their graves holding onto the secrets of who fired those shots that day.

'My grandad told me that both of my great grandads would have been part of the local IRA and may have knocked the bridge that night back in November 1920 and he told me that there is a distinct possibility that great grandads' of some of my classmates may have been some of the men who had fired shots at them, but all those men have now gone to their graves holding onto the secrets of who fired those shots that day.'

Daniel Noonan
Togher National School.

My Grandad Daniel Noonan telling me the story of Pol na barrai bridge.

Kevin Dart O'Flynn
Scoil Eoin National School, Innishannon.

I would like to Say a big thank you to my Grandad Jim for Giving me all this iformation

Proud to hear all about it

I got all this information from my grandmother who is pictured above, left, with her grandfather and her sister.

My grandmother was lucky to have a Memoir written by her father telling her all of the above history and I am lucky and proud to hear all about it now.

She told me that she adored her grandfather; he took her to her first circus, bought her a big book of fairy tales which he used to read aloud to her, dressed up as Santa Claus and made everything fun for her and all his other grandchildren.

Liadhain Ní hÓgáin
Scoil Naomh Bhríde, Union Hall.

Survived that stuff

It was a very troubled time in Ireland and lucky my Great Grandad survived that stuff

Alice Barrett
Scoil Naomh Seosamh, Laragh.

Katie Scannell
St Joseph's GNS, Skibbereen.

Grandad and I chilling half way through our interview.

My great grand father grew up in Gearragh, Rossmore, Clonakilty Co. Cork, where he attended school, & Michael Collins also attended this school!

Éadaoin Kelly
Bandonbridge National School.

Only three of the 11 people that were killed were remembered on this monument—makes you wonder about the other innocent civilians who were killed on that day going about their normal daily tasks. While we look back on these troubled times lets think about the innocent people and thank God for peace in Ireland.

Fiona Twohig
Scoil Mhaoilíosa, Knockavilla.

Momo Sheehy
Gurraneasig National School.

How much more war and hatred, pain and anger do we need in a world that will never be perfect, never be perfect, but can always be changed for good, if only people, realize that you have one life and you do not want to live it quenching happiness and spilling blood.

War is like a piece of food falling in a dirty place and somebody thinking, "If I lick it, it will become clean so I can eat it".

Lucija Kluzniak Madajczak
Abbeystrewry National School, Skibbereen.

Thank you

we would like to acknowledge and most sincerely thank :

Mr. Con O'Callaghan, The Mall, Leap

For his time and information that he so willingly and freely gave

Also :

His wife Marie, for her warm hospitality and beautiful refreshments she served when our minds had reached saturation point!!!

James & Catherine O'Callaghan
Leap National School.

Sam Kingstone
Coolkellure
Dunmanway
Co. Cork

by Caoimhe Gottstein
Derrinacahara N.S.

Caoimhe Gottstein
Derrinacahara National School.

tankes for telling me the story if i win the prize I will give you some. thanks cillian.

Cillian Cuffe
Gurrane National School.

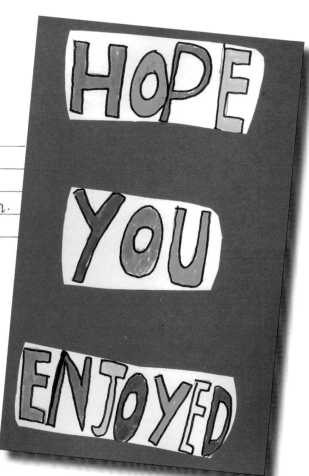

Sophie O'Sullivan
St Joseph's National School, Dromore.

Chapter 14

PARTICIPANTS' NAMES

Abbeystrewry National School, Skibbereen.
Participated 2017

Alanna French
Amy Jennings
Aoife Hendy
Beatrice Attridge
Bryan Jiji John
Byron O'Sullivan
Cayetana McCarthy
Ciarán Coombes
Connor Cuthbertson
Dáthig Finnerty
Emily McMahon
Fionn Coombes
Foyinsolami Aba
Gavin Sweetnam
Gemma Salter
Gráinne O'Donnell
Hal Somerville
Hazel Deane
Hetty Gazzaniga
Isabella O'Sullivan
Leah Cuthbertson
Lucija Kluzniak Madajczak
Mary Swanton
Matthew Benn
Max Tubb
Muireann O'Donnell
Naomi Evans
Naomi Sweetnam
Nori Kluzniak Madajczak
Oran Roycroft
Ross Hendy
Scott Fuller
Stuart Fuller

Ardagh Boy's National School.
Participated 2020

Aleks Kudlacik
Ciarán Campell
Cormac Ó Donnabháin
Danny Sutton
Evan O'Mahony
Gavin Anderson
Jan Ó Longphuirt
Kevin Duffy
Lewis Timmins
Michael McCarthy
Pádraig Tobin
Piotr Samulik
Ryan Collins
Séamus Lane
Seán Cuinnea
Seán Sheehy
Tom Browne

Ardfield National School.
Participated 2020

Aaron White & Jack Barry
Cian O'Donovan
Erin Pettit Mee
Felix Winkelmann
Holly Murray
Mia & Nathan O'Sullivan
Olan Brazier Scannell
Shannon Griffin

Ballinacarriga National School.
Participated 2017

Áine O'Donnell, Michelle O'Donovan & Nicola Nyhan
Caoimhe O'Donovan
Ciara O'Driscoll
Eirinn Duggan
Emily O'Shea
Fergus Murphy
Finian Hurley
Hazel Healy
Hollie Anne Lyons
Isabelle Lehane
Jack Hennigan
Jason Howard
Katie O'Mahony
Luke McCarthy
Maebh O'Brien
Patrick Collins
Peggy McCarthy
Rino Di Rollo
Ryan Collins
Saorla O'Callaghan

Ballinadee National School.
Participated 2018

Aaron Deasy
Abbie McCarthy
Aidan Crowley
Andrea Straub
Carly Helbrow
Ciara O'Donoghue
Ciara White
Colum Morgan
Conor Clifford
Diarmuid Corcoran
David Hickey
Eve & Laura Whitehead & Lauren Crowley
Isabelle Lonergan, Ava McCarthy, Claudia Harrington & Martha Coakley
John Paul McSweeney
Leah Collins
Lisa Neld and Peter Lawlor
Lucy Mulhall
Luke O'Leary
Lydia O'Sullivan
Martha Coakley
Michael Kennedy
Micheál Maguire
Seán Collins
Seán Hales
Sinéad O'Leary

Bandonbridge National School.
Participated 2018

Éadaoin Kelly
Niamh Langford
Ruth Fair

Caheragh National School.
Participated 2017

Alaia O'Sullivan
Alannah Crowley
Amy McKennedy
Caitríona Keohane
Cathail and Emma Hegarty
Cathal O'Sullivan
Christina Hurley
Conan Farrell
Conor Crowley
Danny O'Sullivan
Donal and Caitriona O'Neill
Elaine O'Sullivan
Eleanor Keating
Emma O'Donovan
Eva O'Sullivan
Jamie Crowley
Jason Hurley
Julia Cotter
Katie Daly
Laura Kingston
Louise Keohane
Maeve Kingston
Margaret Collins
Marie O'Sullivan
Maureen Keating
Neil O'Sullivan
Niamh O'Donovan
Nóra O'Driscoll
Peter O'Mahony
Rory Kingston
Shane O'Grady
Shauna McCarthy
Steven Harrington
Teagan Cash
Timothy Farrell

Abbey Cemetary

Abbey Caverly
Kilcoe National School.

Róisín Curtin
Scoil Eoin National School, Innishannon.

Dromleigh National School.
Winning school 2019

Billy Dromey
Caoimhe Shiels
Ciara Bradley
Cillian & Eamon Cronin
Claire & Ella Dromey
Clíona Burgoyne
David O'Riordan
Dylan Lynch
Eve Murphy & Orlagh McBride
Jerry & Daniel O'Riordan
Kristian Cermak
Lucia Duarte
Muireann Kerry
Noah Ryan
Róisín & Tommy Carroll
Saoirse & Seán O'Leary
Sáorlaith Murphy
Sophie Harrington
Tom & Jack Browne

Castledonovan National School.
Participated 2019

Colm O'Regan
Daniel McCarthy
Darragh McCarthy
Emily Hurley
Ethan Hurley
Fionn O'Reilly
Kathlyn McCarthy
Luke Hayes
Matthew Hurley
Phoebe Pettit O'Leary
Romy Pettit O'Leary
Sienna Pettit O'Leary

Coppeen National School.
Participated 2019

Aoibheann O'Driscoll
Caolán O'Donovan
Diarmuid O'Driscoll
Fionn O'Shea
Geraldine McCarthy
Grace Murphy
Liam Collins
Matt Daly
Miah Heffernan
Molly Hilliard
Niamh O'Callaghan

Derrinacahara National School.
Participated 2018

Ashling O'Sullivan
Caoimhe Gottstein
Denis & Shauna Keane
Katie Duggan
Keith McCarthy
Laura Kingston
Michael Kearney
Nina O'Donovan
Sarah Whitehead

Derryclough National School.
Participated 2017

Aidan Connolly,
& illustrated by Nikki
Noonan & Marcus Adams
Lisa O'Donovan

Dreeny National School.
Participated 2020

Adam & Dylan O'Donovan
Alan Beamish
Colin Kingston
Ella O'Sullivan
Grace Kingston
Jack & Tadg Crowley
Jonathan O'Neill
Katie Kingston
Sam Kingston
Shane, Alison & Orla Deane

Drimoleague National School.
Participated 2019

Adam Lordan
Akvile Vaitkute
Alannah Keane
Alex Coughlan
Aoibhinn Twomey
Ben Coughlan
Brianna McCarthy
Chloe & Caoimhe O'Donovan
Chloe Cadogan
Ciaran McSweeney
Cillian Keane
Clara O'Driscoll
Conor Daly
David O' Driscoll
Emily Collins
Emily Dullea
Finn Brickley
Holly Brickley
Jenna O'Dwyer
Kayla Collins
Liam Daly
Lilly O'Driscoll
Lucy Jane O'Driscoll
Marcus O'Riordan
Michael Collins
Natasha O'Donoghue
Niamh O'Reilly
Ryan O'Donovan
Stephen Kingston
Tommy Hurley
Vincent Keane

Gaelscoil Dhochtúir Uí Shúilleabháin, An Sciobairín.
Participated 2017

Ailíse O'Sullivan
Ciara Nic Cormaic
Daniel Greenham Taylor
Dylan MacMahon
Ewan Stuart
Isabel Nic Suibhne
James Ó Coileáin
Jamie Ryan
Jim O'Halloran
Joe Granaghan
Kaya Wild
Lara Nic Suibhne
Louise Ní Mhuireáin
Orna Ní Bhriain
Rowan Ó Leathlaoibhir
Tadhg Ó Treasaigh
Thalia McGuigan

Gaelscoil Dhroichead na Banndan.
Participated 2018

Ava Ní Throithigh
Críostóir Ó Caoinleáin
Cian Ring
Clár Ní Ríordáin
Conchúr Paghan
Daisy Bean
Daniel Ó hAoláin
Daithí Craobhach
Doireann Ní Cheallaigh
Ella Seamlaír
Ída Ní Aodha
Jack Ó Murchú
Jean Ní Dhonnabháin
Martha Ní Dhonnabháin
Michael O'Donovan
Micheál Ó Conraí
Muireann Nic Pháidín
Rachel Ní Chatháin
Saoirse Ní Dhonnchú
Stíofán Tóibín
Zoe Lawlor

Gaelscoil Mhichíl Uí Choileáin, Clonakilty.
Winning school 2020

Aran Ó Céilleachair
Andrew & Flor Mac Cárthaigh
Darragh Ó Mathúna
Derry Ó Donnabháin
Éanna Déiseach
Freya Scott
Gabrielle Nic Chárthaigh-Ní Néill
Jasmine Ní Oistín
Kadi Deasy
Lilah Stíobhard
Lily O'Donnell Bradley (winning pupil)
Molly Boddington & Niamh Hilliard
Molly Ní Chinnseabháin
Noel Mac Fhinn
Realtín Deli
Tadhg Ó Seighin
Tomás Mac Giolla Phádraig

Gurrane National School.
Participated 2018

Adam Lynch
Anna Collins
Callum Reardon
Caoimhe Craig
Cillian Cuffe
Jack O'Sullivan

Gurraneasig National School.
Participated 2018

Ava Madden
Cash Healy
Grace O'Neill
Layla O'Neill
Momo Sheehy
Torin O'Kennedy
Zach Allen

Kilbrittain National School
Participated 2018

Chloe Coughlan
John Ryan
Karol Egan
Kylie O'Donovan
Lisa-Marie O'Connor
Shay Fehilly O'Brien
Tom Warner

Kilcoe National School.
Participated 2019

Abbey Caverly
Emer Caverly
Leah Carey
Maebh Collins
Mia Boucher

Kilcolman National School.
Participated 2018

Annabel Tapia
Aoife Galvin
Aoife O'Flynn Meade
Donnagh O' Driscoll
Ellie Hosford
Emma Galvin
Emer Moroney
Gary Lordan
Gavin Nyhan
Madison Sullivan
Milo Forsey
Míde O h-Icí
Orlaith O'Flynn Meade
Sam & Ben Jones
Shane O'Hare
Síofra Hegarty

Kilgarriffe National School.
Participated 2020

Ada Sadowska
Amon Papasang
Isabel Codd
Jonah Sutton
Liana Cirule
Lucie Bradley
Matthew Buttimer
Nicholas Deane
Oisín O'Callaghan-Platt
William Kingston
Zoe McInerney

Knockskeagh National School.
Participated 2020

Annie McCarthy
Ciara Murphy
Claire Scanlon
Clodagh O'Regan
Donnchadh Keohane
Joe Coleman
Joshua & Emily Williamson
Kerry Coombes
Matthew Draper
Mattie Coffey
May Gaynor
Meghan Coakley
Poppy Buttimer
Seán Finn

Leap National School.
Winning school 2017

Ava Scarlett
Cathal O'Driscoll
Conor Burns
Gavin Collins & Sophie O'Donovan
Jade Philpott
James & Catherine O'Callaghan
Joseph Mahon
Kate Connolly
Katie Coughlan
Kinga and Robert Szylko
Luke and Leon Curley
Mark Cooke
Raonaid Kerrisk
Seán O'Driscoll

Lisavaird National School.
Participated 2020

Cathal Buchanan
Cathal O'Leary
Conor and Liam Dooley
David O'Sullivan
Dylan Scannell
Eoghan O'Keeffe
Gemma O'Sullivan
Grace Hourihane
Karol McCarthy
Matthew Harrington
Ryan Fitzpatrick
Uinseann O'Mahony

Lisheen National School.
Participated 2017

Aidan O'Dwyer
Alannah Cawley
Anna Hurley
Bláthín Barry
Chloe O'Mahony
Conor Casey
Daniel Hurley
Edwin Collins
Eoghan Cawley
Ferdia Dennis-McAleavy
John & James Hurley
Kate Hurley
Kyle O'Sullivan
Lydia Dwyer
Molly Casey
Oisin Cooke
Riona O'Driscoll
Shauna O'Driscoll

Rathmore National School.
Participated 2017

Anna-Sofie Haffner
Colm Harrington
Eleanor Pavry
Ellie O'Driscoll
Emma & Ellen Hurley
Fionn O'Connor
Gráinne Connolly
Harry Bushe
John Kearney
Johnny Walsh
Keelin Murphy
Kevin Harte
Lachlan O'Regan
Liam & Dan Connolly
Niamh Connolly
Qhairun Sofea Binti Anuar
Richard Bushe
Ryan O'Driscoll
Saoirse O'Donovan Kirwan
Sarah Connolly
Seamus Griffiths
Tomek Lechtanski

Reenascreena National School.
Participated 2020

Aobh Daly
Caleb O'Donovan
Cillian Forsythe
Eloise Fitzpatrick
Fionn Fargnoli
Annie McCarthy
Jason O'Shea
John O'Donovan
Naomi Harding
Seán Forsythe
Wayne McCarthy

Ethan McNamara
Scoil na mBuachaillí, Clonakilty.

S.N. Rath A' Bharraigh/ Rathbarry National School.
Participated 2020

Anna Brinkmann
Cathal O'Donovan
Daniel O'Mahony
Daniel, Euan & Kate Whelton
Éabha O'Leary
Laura Deasy
Rory O'Donovan

Scoil Bhríde National School, Ballydehob.
Participated 2019

Anna Cronin
Anna Sheehan
Caroline Harrington
Cíla O'Connor
Conor Coughlan
Dara Seegers
Ella Camier
Ellen O'Donovan
Eveanna Goulding
Gearoid Coughlan
Gracie Sidaway
James Hodgson
Jennifer McCarthy
Joe Melvin Caird
Liam Coughlan
Lucy & Daniel Copithone
Marcal Kottler
Matthew Duggan
Micah Simpson
Oliva Killeen
Thomas Hodnett

Scoil Eoin National School, Innishannon.
Winning school 2018

Abbie Atkinson
Adam O'Sullivan
Aidan Davison
Áine O'Brien
Amy Barry
Anthony Slattery
Ashlee Madden
Billa (Daniel) Kelleher Barry
Calum O'Driscoll
Charlie Callanan
Chloe Kelly
Chloe McCarthy
Ciarán Brady
Conor Nash
Croíona Murphy
Daniel Healy
Diarmuid Brady
Donagh Shiels
Éabha Murphy
Eddie O'Sullivan
Ella Ryan
Ellie Keane
Fia Callanan
Grace O'Leary
Hugo Woods
Jack Brew
Jack McCarthy
Kate McEntee
Kate Morrissey
Keelin Holland
Kevin Dart O'Flynn (winning pupil 2018)
Killian McCarthy
Lemor Carreon
Liam Fitzgerald
Louis O'Sullivan
Lydia Huggard
Mathew Kelleher
Meadhbh Kiely
Millie Slyne
Naomi O'Sullivan
Nicholas Curtin
Róisín Curtin
Ruth Motherway
Samuel Linehan
Sophie O'Sullivan
Sorcha Hurley
Sorcha Kiely
Suzie Murphy
Tara O'Farrell

Scoil Mhaoilíosa, Knockavilla.
Participated 2018

Abbie O'Sullivan
Adam Barnemann
Aileen Lynch
Alan Madden
Alex Hurley
Aoife O'Donovan
Ava Cullinane
Billy Cronin
Bobby Lynch
Callum Fennelly
Cara O'Sullivan
Cian O'Mahony
Ciara Dullea
Danny O'Brien
Fiona Twohig
Gary Cremin
Kate O'Sullivan
Matthew Hoban
Megan O'Kane
Mia Kelleher
Muireann McCarthy
Paul Madden
Ruby Murphy
Seán O'Connor
Shane Ryan
Syakira Ulmann

Scoil Mhuire National School, Schull.
Participated 2019

Áine Méabh O'Regan
Amy Wilde
Billy O'Connor
Charlie Lannin
Christina Robb
Dermot Ward
Edward O'Sullivan
Evan Dukelow
Finn Bueb
Fintan O'Brien
Killian Power
Kiva Scannell
Liadh O'Donovan
Louis Dolan Anderson
Ryan O'Driscoll
Sasha Sahous
Shane Crowley
Shauna Stam

Ethan McNamara
Scoil na mBuachaillí, Clonakilty.

Scoil na mBuachaillí, Clonakilty.
Participated 2020

Alex Aherne
Alex Gawel
Alex O'Regan
Darragh Murphy
Eoghan Minihan
Etaoin Mulcahy
Ethan McNamara
Finn O'Mahony
Harry Hayes
James Maguire
Lennart Lindenfeld
Louis Kelleher
Mattie Lyons
Michael Francis Collins
Nicholas Lendacky
Peadar Dinneen
Peter O'Mahoney
Phillip Perrichon
Rohan Horgan
Shourya Malik

Scoil Náisiúnta Inis Chléire
Participated 2017

Alex Cocking & Sorcha Lucioli
Freya Affleck Keogh
Katy & Rowan Thomas
Molly Cadogan
Shane Langley
Zemi Perry

Scoil Naomh Bhríde, Union Hall.
Participated 2017

Ailbhe Dahm
Aisling Forde
Ben Perez
Callum Moloney
Daisy Taylor
Davin Limrick
Donal O'Callaghan
Jack Moloney
Kate Connolly
Kellie Daly
Kellie Pearce
Liadhain Ní hÓgáin
Lucy Deasy
Paddy French
Paddy French, Sarah McCarthy &
Liadhain Hogan
Yasmin Atalay

Scoil Naomh Seosamh, Laragh, Bandon.
Participated 2018

Aislinn O'Riordan
Alice Barrett
Aoife Callanan
Caoimhe Foley
Caoimhe Lehane
Christine & Ellen Culloty
Ciara McCarthy
Cormac O'Flynn
Maebh Doyle, Hannah France
& Niamh Quinlan
Jay Brennan
Jenny Fleming
Kayla Mulcahy
Meabh O'Mahony
Oisín McQuaid Scahill
Rachael Gaffney

Scoil Phádraig Naofa, Bandon
Participated 2018

Donncha McCarthy
Ronan Crowley

Scoil Phádraig Naofa, Dunmanway.
Participated 2019

Adam Barry
Eoin Hurley (winning pupil
2019)
Euan Lehane
Liam Henry Kearney
Ian Martin
Jamie Dullea
John Smyth
Killian Collins
Matthew O'Neill
Michael Sheehan
Nathan McCarthy
Niall Owens
Ógie Walsh
Ronan White
Shaun O'Connell

St Joseph's Girls National School, Clonakilty.
Participated 2020

Abbie Wedlock
Aisling O'Mahony
Anna Goyal
Ebube Ogwudiegwa
Erin Cahalane
Eva Pattwell
Lucy O'Connell
Meabh O'Mahony
Míscha May Pattwell
Sophie Bell

St Joseph's GNS, Skibbereen.
Participated 2017

Aisling Collins
Amie O'Driscoll
Amy McCarthy
Ayleasha Brosnan
Aoife Hurley
Ava Minihane
Claire Griffin
Elaine O'Donovan
Ellen Marks
Ellen O'Donovan
Ellie McCarthy
Ericka Dempsey
Grace Gallagher
Kate Coppinger
Katie Scannell (winning pupil
2017)
Kayla Scully
Lara O'Donovan
Leah Fitzgerald
Leah Geaney
Lilly Heaton-Jones & Jessie
Holmes
Lisa O'Driscoll
Lucy Bielecki
Mary Whooley & Saoirse Lucey
Mary-Elizabeth Deasy
Michaela Maguire
Molly Lomasney
Rebecca Connolly
Viktorija Stonyte

St Joseph's National School, Dromore.
Participated 2019

Aaron Cadogan
Adam Gilman-Burke
Aoife d'Hondt
Ashan Waseem
Connor Collins
Connor Crowley
Daniel McGrath
Daniel Ward
Darragh Harrington
Darragh O'Regan
Denis Cadogan
Denis Collins
Fintan Cadogan
Gavin O'Sullivan
Greg Mulhall
Jack Moore
John Mulhall
Kita O'Brien
Lisa Buckley
Maria Barry
Nicol Lenczuk
Norah Cronin
Rachel Crowley
Ria Buckley
Saoirse Horgan
Sophie O'Sullivan

St Mary's Primary School, Rosscarbery.
Participated 2020

Anna Connelly
Bonnie Hayes
Caoimhe Murphy
Chloe Ronan
Cíara Tobin
Ellie Curtin
Grace Buckingham
Iseult O'Regan
Meabh Cuinnea
Méabh Ní Dhonnabháin

Eoghan Minihan |
Scoil na mBuachaillí, Clonakilty. |

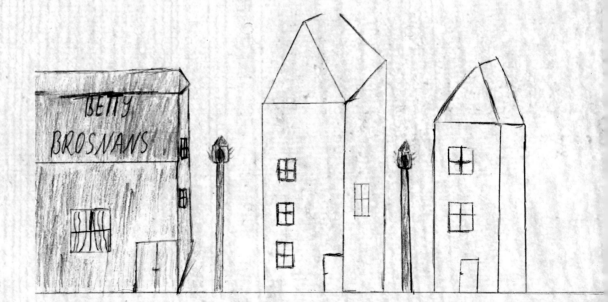

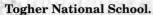

St Mary's Senior School, Dunmanway.
Participated 2019

Abbie Collins
Abbie McCarthy & Laura Dullea
Agata Kalkowska & Sarah White
Aislinn Farr
Alannis Mohan-Sexton
Alex Mawe
Amy Collins, Shannon Murray
& Siobhán Carroll
Aoife Barry
Caoimhe & Maebh McCarthy
Caoimhe Burns
Chloe Lordan
Ciara Burke
Ciara Galvin
Clodagh Mannix
Eimer Martin
Elle Jane Kelleher
Ellie Buckley
Gina Long
Hazel Murphy
Katelyn O'Connell
Katie Cotter
Larissa Farr
Laura Hayes Flynn
Lauren Farr
Leah Kearney
Meave O'Mahony
& Sarah White
Nicola Kearney
Orlaith Crowley
Orlaith Hickey
Sarah Hilliard
Sarah White
Shauna Kelly
Shauna Lordan
Shauna Walsh

St Patrick's BNS, Skibbereen.
Participated 2017

Andrew Scannell
Ciarán Bohane
Daniel Cleary
Eoin O'Sullivan
Jack Grace
Mark Keating
Naoise Quinn
Neil McCarthy

The Model School, Dunmanway.
Participated 2019

Amber Bryan
Anna O'Driscoll
Emma Draper
Killian Kingston
Molly O'Brien
Sara Bryan
Sive Buckley
Tara McCarthy
Tom Sweetnam
Zara Stout

Togher National School.
Participated 2019

Alice O'Donovan
Aoibheann & Shauna Hurley
Clóda Hayes
Connie Noonan
Daniel Noonan
Dara Russell
Fionn, Jason & Liam McCarthy
Kimi & Levi Bosma
Luke Hall
Muiris & Kelly-Ann Buttimer

Abbey Caverly
Kilcoé National School.

Katie Scannell
St Joseph's GNS, Skibbereen.

Mark Cooke
Leap National School.

Stíofán Tóibín
Gaelscoil Dhroichead na Banndan.

Acknowledgements

This project is the culmination of years of work by the Skibbereen Heritage Centre team and involved the participation and support of a very large number of people in West Cork.

First and foremost, a huge thank you to the 823 pupils who contributed with such passion and energy, and to all of those who so generously shared their stories with them. The children's essays are a truly unique and wonderful representation of these events and the interviewees can be justifiably proud of their efforts.

Thanks, also, to the fantastic teachers and staff of the schools who mentored and encouraged the pupils with so much enthusiasm. They really were incredibly helpful, and a joy to work with, and were also very patient with the administration involved.

The project was enabled by funding from the Cork County Council Centenary Programme and we are enormously grateful for the support of both the Centenary Committee members, and Heritage Officer Conor Nelligan. Sincere thanks also to Mac Dara O h-Icí and Niall Healy of Cork County Council for recognising the project's value from the start; and to the Mayor of Cork County, Cllr Gillian Coughlan, for contributing the foreword to this publication. We are also very grateful to Donal O'Driscoll/Access Credit Union for sponsoring the inaugural year prizes.

We would also like to express our sincere and wholehearted appreciation of our colleagues' extraordinary efforts on behalf of this project. This was an enormous task for such a small team — liaising repeatedly with the schools, scanning and archiving the material, as well as cataloguing and uploading it online. A special mention for the schools' co-ordinators, William Casey and Philip O'Regan, for their fantastic work on this project over the years. Thanks also to Sue Harrington for all her help cataloguing and proofing the material; and to Barry McMahon, Saoirse Connolly, Sarah Tighe and Deirdre Collins for their willing and good-humoured support and encouragement — thanks everyone.

A sincere and much-deserved thank you to the very talented Alan Tobin for his superb design work and endless patience — Alan, your contribution is so very much appreciated. And thanks also to Kevin O'Farrell for his wonderful photography and sound advice; and to Patricia & Kevin Tomlinson, Flor MacCarthy, Elaine O'Flynn, Elaine Desmond and Siobhán Cronin for their feedback and astute observations. Agus míle buíochas le Emer Ní Mhurchú as an gcabhair le na haistí Gaeilge and to Seán O'Neill/Union Hall Computers for IT support

The final acknowledgement must go to all those who suffered worldwide during this revolutionary period — this project is in their honour.

Terri Kearney & Margaret Murphy, June 2022.

Gary Lordan
Kilcolman National School.

The Stories of the Revolution Team

Terri Kearney: project instigator/manager.
Margaret Murphy: schools' co-ordinator & administrator 2017–2020.
Philip O'Regan: schools' co-ordinator & administrator 2017–2018.
William Casey: schools' co-ordinator & administrator 2019–2020.
Sue Harrington: administration/cataloguing 2017–2020.
Supported by: Barry McMahon, Saoirse Connolly, Sarah Tighe and Deirdre Collins.

About the Authors

Terri Kearney is a native of Skibbereen and has managed Skibbereen Heritage Centre since it opened in 2000. She has published three books previously: *Lough Hyne: the Marine Researchers in Pictures* (2011), *Lough Hyne: From Prehistory to the Present* (2013), *Skibbereen: The Famine Story* (co-author, 2015) as well as contributing a chapter to *The Presidents' Letters* (2021) by Flor MacCarthy. She has also written articles for the Skibbereen and District Historical Society Journal.

Margaret Murphy, originally from Cork city, has lived in West Cork since 2002 when she joined the Skibbereen Heritage Centre team. An avid genealogist and historian, she has helped thousands of people in search of their Irish ancestry over the years and has also contributed to the Skibbereen and District Historical Journal.

| Caoimhe O'Donovan
| Ballinacarriga National School.

Images inside back cover by:
Emer Moroney, Kilcolman National School | Caoimhe & Maebh McCarthy, St Mary's Senior School, Dunmanway | Caoimhe Foley, Scoil Naomh Seosamh, Laragh | Denis Collins, St Joseph's National School, Dromore | Greg Mulhall, St Joseph's National School, Dromore | Jasmine Ní Oistín, Gaelscoil Mhichíl Uí Choileáin, Clonakilty | Keelin Holland, Scoil Eoin National School, Innishannon | Liadhain Ní hÓgáin, Scoil Naomh Bhríde, Union Hall | Lucia Duarte, Dromleigh National School | Noel Mac Fhinn, Gaelscoil Mhichíl Uí Choileáin, Clonakilty | Ruth Motherway, Scoil Eoin National School, Innishannon | Shay Fehilly O'Brien, Kilbrittain National School | Sorcha Kiely, Scoil Eoin National School, Innishannon | Zoe McInerney, Kilgarriffe National School | Claire & Ella Dromey, Dromleigh National School | William Kingston, Kilgarriffe National School.

This publication has been supported by Cork County Council through its Commemorations Committee and through the support of the Department of Tourism, Culture, Arts, Gaeltacht, Sport and Media.

SKIBBEREEN HERITAGE CENTRE

Comhairle Contae Chorcaí
Cork County Council

An Roinn Turasóireachta, Cultúir, Ealaíon, Gaeltachta, Spóirt agus Meán
Department of Tourism, Culture, Arts, Gaeltacht, Sport and Media

Stories from the Revolution

1916 to 1923

Hitory project.

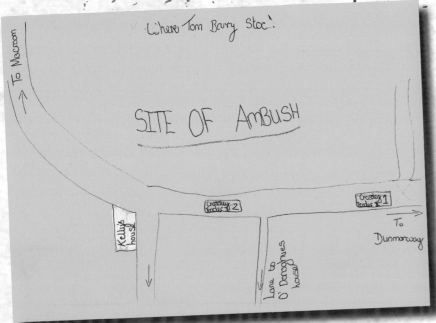

Where Tom Barry Stoo!

To Macroom

SITE OF AMBUSH

Crossley tender 2

Crossley tender 1

Kelly's house

Lane to O'Donoghues house

To Dunmanway

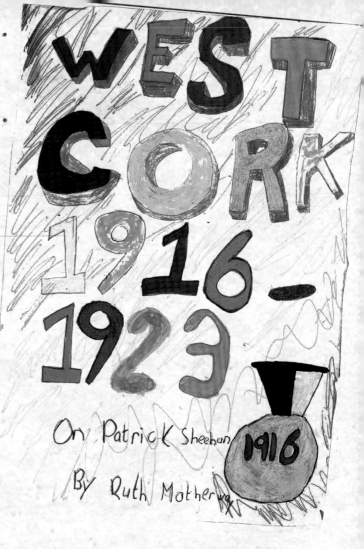

WEST CORK 1916 - 1923

On Patric K Sheehan 1916

By Ruth Motherwa

Thank You For Reading

Guns in the Door Frame

F

W.

7